Contents

Precautions and Perils	7
The Dawn of Darkness	15
Foundations of Demonology	31
The Devil's Dominion	45
Identifying the Infernal	59
Diabolical Diary	71
Deflecting Darkness	87
Infernal Infestations	97
The Possessed and the Purified	113
Legends of the Damned	131
Opening the Gates of Hell	143
A Pact with the Devil	167
Sinister Sanctuaries	179
Dark Hexes and Harm	189
Puppets of Power	201
Unholy Ceremonies	211
Glossary	219

Precautions and Perils

In the dark world of demonology, stern warnings and cautionary notes are not merely suggestions—they are dire necessities. As the essence of demonology has shifted dramatically over the centuries, from the guarded domain of church-sanctioned exorcists to present-day enthusiasts and scholars, we now stand on the precipice of a new era. The ancient superstitions have crumbled, revealing a path fraught with peril and excitement.

While demonology is the study of the demonic, the branch of demonology covered in this book goes deeper and much darker. Dabbling with the occult, summoning demons, and tampering with forces beyond human comprehension is a form of black magic. It is fundamentally a selfish perversion of the mystical arts that involves the deliberate use of rituals and spells to achieve personal power, to destroy others, or to gain control over people and supernatural entities. Unlike their counterparts who practice white magic, black magicians often make pacts with malevolent entities, including the Devil himself, to achieve their aims.

To summon a demon is to invite chaos into your life. These malevolent entities are not bound by the moral codes or whims of humanity. They are ancient, cunning, and infinitely patient, waiting for the perfect moment to strike. Engaging with such forces can lead to a cascade of dire consequences, each more harrowing than the last.

Make no mistake, demons are exceedingly dangerous entities. Summoning demons is not a game. If you call them forth, you must be prepared to send them back.

Tales of people being pushed, scratched, or struck by malevolent spirits abound, while those who are haunted by demons often spiral into violence, depression, and despair—sometimes even to the brink of suicide.

One of the most immediate risks is possession. Demons seek to infiltrate and dominate, eroding the will of their victims until nothing remains but a shell of their former selves. Possession can manifest in myriad ways: drastic changes in personality, uncontrollable fits of rage, physical contortions, and an overwhelming sense of despair. The possessed may lose all sense of self, their actions driven by the malevolent force that has taken hold.

Even if a victim escapes the clutches of possession, the residual effects can be devastating. Persistent nightmares, hallucinations, and an unshakable feeling of being watched are common afflictions. The mental toll can lead to paranoia, anxiety, and a descent into madness, as the boundary between reality and the demonic blurs. These entities thrive on fear and suffering, drawing strength from the anguish they inflict.

Furthermore, summoning rituals often require the use of dangerous artefacts and forbidden knowledge. The ancient texts and grimoires that contain these rituals are fraught with cryptic instructions and dire warnings, their true meanings obscured by time and translation. Misinterpretation is a constant threat, with a single mispronounced word or misplaced symbol capable of unleashing untold horrors.

Incorrectly performed rituals can result in unintended negative consequences. This backlash can manifest as personal misfortune, deterioration of your mental state, or even physical harm. Engaging in demonic practices often involves making morally questionable decisions, such as harming others or entering into pacts with malevolent entities. This can lead to a gradual erosion of ethical boundaries and a descent into further malevolence.

There is also the risk of opening a portal or gateway to the infernal realm, a breach through which other malevolent entities can enter our realm. Such breaches can disrupt the natural order, causing disturbances that attract even more sinister forces. These portals can be exceedingly difficult to close, leaving the summoner and those around them vulnerable to continual assaults from the beyond.

As a seasoned demonologist, I have spent decades immersed in the study and practice of various magical arts. The rituals and practices described herein are not to be taken lightly. They are fraught with danger and can be catastrophic for individuals who are mentally unstable or otherwise not in a sound state of mind. Individuals who are not mentally stable or are in poor psychological health are particularly vulnerable. The rituals can exacerbate existing conditions, leading to confusion and mental breakdowns.

If you are weak in mind and spirit, demons will exploit your vulnerabilities, making you feel possessed, tormented, and consumed by terror. However, for those of you with the strength and resolve, this book will help you traverse the treacherous terrain of demonology, where the rewards can be significant, but they come at a price. Belief and intent are critical components in magical practices.

If you harbour any serious doubts about demonology, turn back now. This is not a field for the faint-hearted or the conflicted. Those whose religious beliefs clash with the study of demons should avoid this path, as it can lead to profound guilt and inner turmoil.

This book is not intended for skeptics; their disbelief will only hinder their progress and understanding. By nature, skeptics doubt the existence or efficacy of supernatural phenomena, which can influence the outcomes of such rituals. A lack of faith in the process may negate any potential effects, rendering the rituals ineffective. Therefore, those who approach black magic must do so with unwavering conviction, understanding that it is deliberate manipulation of magical forces and the conscious decision to employ these dark arts for nefarious purposes.

Heed this warning: In essence, meddling with the occult and summoning demons is an invitation to darkness and despair. The risks are not merely theoretical—they are based on countless accounts throughout history and contemporary experiences. Those who tread this path do so at their own peril, courting forces that cannot be controlled or fully understood. Proceed with caution, and may your journey into the depths of demonology be both enlightening and empowering, as it has been for me.

In nomine Dei nostri Satanas Luciferi excelsi. In the name of Satan, the ruler of the Earth, the king of the world, I command the forces of darkness to bestow their infernal power upon me. Open wide the gates of Hell and come forth from the abyss to greet me as your brother/sister and friend.

The Dawn of Darkness

My journey into the paranormal began at the tender age of five, in the heart of South London. I remember waking up in the middle of the night in my mum's tiny terraced house. I walked through the living room to the scullery, where there was a mangle. I opened the door to get a drink of water, and there, behind the mangle, I saw somebody's arm moving. That's all I remember. That was the first weird thing that happened to me.

Almost ten years later, I was walking around Belgrave Square with some friends and noticed the Spiritualist Association of Great Britain. Despite knowing nothing about it, I walked in. The building was full of photos of famous people after they'd died, and the association had tape recordings of them speaking from beyond the grave. I thought it sounded interesting, but I didn't really believe a word of it. Then I started looking into it further.

This exploration led me to the world of demonology, the field I now specialise in and a topic I have researched in depth over the years. Demons are said to be fallen angels that God cast out because they were no good— they were horrible, bad angels. The concept of demons goes back thousands of years and can be found in Egyptian mythology, as well as pretty much every religion and culture around the world. If you believe in

God, you have to believe in the Devil and demons because they both go together. You can't have one without the other.

Despite the fact that demons are rooted in so many different cultures and religions, my Western approach to demonology keeps me safe. I've only come across demons I've called up, unless one comes through accidentally. In such cases, I call up another one to get rid of it. That's the way I work.

My expertise in demons and the paranormal led me to an encounter with Yvette Fielding and the 'Most Haunted' team when they came to investigate the eerie occurrences at my stunning Grade II listed home. The Clock House, nestled deep in the Surrey Hills, with its 12th-century origins, has a long history of paranormal activity that intrigued both the show's investigators and its viewers.

There's a corridor upstairs where you can smell roses at one time of the year and lavender at another. These smells are commonly associated with the paranormal, indicating the presence of someone. There are a couple of rooms on the third floor that feel strange, where a couple of children died due to illness. Other reported paranormal activity includes the ghosts of two monks seen in the ground-floor corridor, ghostly footsteps on the upper floor, a door that opens and closes on its own, and the ghost of a woman wearing a bonnet. I know exactly who these spirits were, as I have records of all the house's owners going back to 1207.

Guests who have stayed at my house have reported waking up in the night and seeing a figure wearing a distinctive hat, the type worn by a beadle, standing near their bed. A beadle, a church official, used to live in the house.

The investigation at the Clock House aired in July 2003 on Living TV, marking my first appearance on the show. It was here that Derek Acorah, the show's medium, unveiled a series of astonishing revelations. He sensed the presence of a soldier from the Knights Templar and a priest hidden within a priest hole, which had once been a sanctuary during times of religious persecution.

I shared my own experiences, including a photograph I had taken that appeared to show a ghostly form in the living room. The show's paranormal investigator, Phil Whyman, validated the image, describing the capture as an "ectoplasmic mist." Derek also made a startling declaration: I might be the reincarnation of Baron De Rizzbregg, a former resident of the house from the 14th century. This revelation explained the spirits' apparent satisfaction with my renovations.

The investigation took a dramatic turn when Derek identified a female spirit named Ruth, whom he said followed me from my London nightclub, Caesar's. This revelation set the stage for the team's subsequent investigation at the club.

A week later, 'Most Haunted' delved into the spectral secrets of Caesar's Nightclub. This establishment, rich in history and transformation, had become infamous for its paranormal activity. From its days as a grand ballroom in 1928 to its modern incarnation as a nightclub, it had seen it all. Yet, it was the spirit of Ruth Ellis, the last woman hanged in England, who haunted its halls and my thoughts.

During the investigation, the team experienced an array of unexplained phenomena. Eerie noises echoed through the dressing rooms, and a palpable sense of unease permeated the air. Despite our best efforts to capture substantial evidence, we only managed to document fleeting glimpses of the paranormal, including a brief flash of light when Karl Beattie called out to Ruth Ellis.

Following my initial series two appearance, Living TV sought someone versed in witchcraft, and I confidently stepped forward, leading to my participation in several 'Most Haunted Live!' shows. One of the most memorable was the Village of the Damned in Wales, a seven-night special broadcast from Denbigh Asylum over Halloween in 2008. Thrust into the deep end, I conducted an interview with Julian Clegg before an audience of 1,000 people. It was a defining moment, solidifying my place within the 'Most Haunted' family.

During the live specials, I spent a lot of time on stage with Paul Ross and our historian, Lesley Smith. Gradually, I transitioned into the series, and, since 2014, I've been the show's resident demonologist, giving the show a darker, edgier dimension.

As a demonologist, I often recite incantations to summon or communicate with dark forces. These verses, many derived from the Satanic Bible, are powerful and dangerous. The show's audio levels are often lowered during the broadcast of these recitations to prevent viewers from replicating them, ensuring the incantations remain a guarded secret.

My first regular appearance was during the exploration of the Royal Court Theatre in Bacup, which aired in August 2014. The Royal Court Theatre, with its rich and storied past, proved to be a hotspot for paranormal activity. From the basement's knocking sounds to the scent of perfume and objects being hurled, the investigation was a whirlwind of unexplained phenomena. Alongside the team, I conducted vigils, set trigger objects, and even performed a séance using a Ouija board, during which we communicated with a spirit named Jake—a familiar presence from previous investigations.

Annison Funeral Parlour was one of the most eerie locations we visited. This place had a grim history, once serving as a funeral home where countless bodies were prepared for their final journey. The atmosphere was thick with the energy of its past.

During my lone vigil on the mortuary slab, I called upon the dark entities that might still linger in this place. I recited incantations to summon and communicate with these spirits. The room was deathly silent as I began, "In nomine Dei nostri Satanas Luciferi excelsi, come forth from the shadows and reveal yourselves to me."

The air grew heavy, and a palpable sense of dread filled the room. Suddenly, there was a loud bang, as if something had been thrown across the room. I could feel the temperature dropping, a common sign of a spirit's presence. Despite the fear that any normal person would feel, I remained focused, continuing my incantations, "I invite the forces of darkness to bestow their infernal power upon me. Show yourselves and make your presence known."

The most intense moment came when I felt an overwhelming heat enveloping the mortuary slab. It was as if the energy of the departed was converging on that spot. I closed the vigil with a final command, "Depart from this place in peace, return to your rest." The experience was profound and provided undeniable evidence of the paranormal activity in Annison Funeral Parlour.

Another memorable moment occurred during our filming at Knottingley Town Hall in Yorkshire, where I conducted one of the most controversial experiments of my career —a voodoo ritual targeting one of our crew members, Stuart Torevell. The history of the town hall, built on the remains of a medieval monastery and used for witchcraft and pagan rituals, made it an ideal location for this experiment.

I created a voodoo doll using traditional methods, including personal items from Stuart, to establish a connection. As I began the ritual in the dark cellar, I recited, "By the power vested in this doll, I command the spirit to manifest in Stuart's body. Let him feel the presence of the dark forces that reside here."

Unbeknownst to Stuart, he was upstairs participating in a Ouija board session with the team. The moment I inserted a pin into the doll's right arm, Stuart reacted visibly, clutching his arm in pain. He described the sensation as a sharp, sudden pain, as if something had pierced his skin.

I continued, placing pins in his left arm and legs, each time observing Stuart's reactions via the synced cameras. His discomfort was clear, and when I covered the doll's eyes, Stuart reported his vision becoming impaired, "I can't see, all my vision's impaired. I honestly can't see. I can't see a thing."

This experiment was not without controversy. While some viewed it as undeniable proof of the paranormal, others remained skeptical. Regardless, it showcased the potential power of voodoo and my ability to connect with the dark forces that inhabit these haunted locations.

Each location we visited brought its own unique challenges and spectral inhabitants, but only one resulted in a brush with pure evil—a place that has haunted my thoughts ever since and my proudest moment with the show. We spent four nights in the Czech Republic town of Prague shooting a 'Most Haunted: Live!' event titled 'Gothic Prague: Evil Within' in 2010.

On the final night, we visited Houska Castle, but this isn't just any castle—it is the only place in the world where the Devil is said to have appeared from a hole in the ground. The legends, the sinister history, and the palpable malevolence make it a place like no other.

Castle Houska, built by Cistercian monks, was not constructed as a residence. Its sole purpose was to seal a terrifying gateway to Hell. In 878 AD, the entrance to Satan's lair supposedly cracked open, and bizarre half-human beasts and flying creatures spewed forth. The castle, especially its chapel, was built over this gaping hole to imprison the evil within. It wasn't built to keep people out; it was built to keep something in.

Inside the castle, a fresco depicts a unique devilish creature, unlike anything seen elsewhere, except perhaps in the 'Codex Gigas', 'The Devil's Bible'. This artwork shows Archangel Michael, the leader of the heavenly army, battling with demons. The castle's very walls seemed to whisper of the horrors contained within.

During our investigation, the team locked me in the chapel. I began my incantations in Latin, calling out to Satan. The atmosphere was thick with malevolence; you could cut the evil with a knife. As I chanted, my briefcase toppled over, and papers were pulled out individually by unseen forces. This moment, caught on camera, was terrifying, but I felt an overwhelming presence. I thought, "He's here, I've got him."

Despite the activity around me, I continued with my incantations, pushing through the fear, driven by the dark energy that surrounded me. I was convinced that I was on the verge of coming face-to-face with Satan himself. But just as the air thickened with anticipation, the production team intervened, calling an end to the vigil. That's the closest I've ever come to him, and it left an indelible mark on my soul.

Castle Houska's sinister reputation is further darkened by its history under German occupation during World

War II. Adolf Hitler, fascinated by the occult, assigned General Reinhard Heydrich to the castle. The Nazis were known for their interest in black magic, and I believe their occupation of the castle was not just for tactical advantage but also for what lay beneath it. The dark forces that have always been imprisoned within those ancient walls.

My experience at Houska Castle remains the most profound and dangerous encounter I've ever had. The evil that resides there is real, and it is a place where the line between our world and the demonic blurs. It's a reminder that some doors, once opened, should never be closed.

My appearances on 'Most Haunted' led to the opportunity to host events and go ghost hunting with the public, something that is always an exhilarating experience, especially at a location as rich in history and hauntings as Charlton House in Greenwich. In 2021, we had one such memorable night, and it yielded some extraordinary evidence of the paranormal.

During the event at this magnificent Grade I listed Jacobean manor, one of the participants captured a photograph that sent chills down everyone's spine. The image shows a dark, shadowy figure standing on the Minstrel's Gallery wearing a three-cornered hat that has no legs. The photo was nothing short of brilliant, but undeniably scary.

For those who have seen me on screen or come on a ghost hunt with me, you will know I am never without my crucifix—a large, mirrored Mexican cross—and a large, locking leather journal filled with parchment. These items have become my trademark, symbols of my quest to confront and document the supernatural. The question I am asked most frequently is, "What is in your book?"

Well, in this book, I will finally share the secrets that have been locked away in my journal. It is a compendium of ancient incantations, spells, and rituals, carefully documented over years of study and practice. These are not mere scribblings; they are powerful invocations that can summon, bind, and banish the darkest of entities.

I have always been drawn to the dark, the mysterious, and the shadows that lurk at the edge of our understanding. It is this fascination that led me to the 'Codex Gigas', a tome whispered about in hushed tones and revered as much as it is feared. When I decided to pen this book, there was no doubt in my mind about what it should be called: 'The Devil's Bible'. The name itself evokes a shiver, a primal fear, and it is precisely that sensation I wish to explore.

The 'Codex Gigas', the original Devil's bible, is a medieval manuscript unlike any other. Bound in the early 13th century in the Benedictine monastery of Podlažice in Bohemia, it is a monstrous volume, both in size and in the weight of its legends. Measuring nearly a metre in height and weighing as much as a full-grown man, it stands as a testament to human endeavour—and perhaps something far darker.

The heart of the Codex Gigas is its unsettling, full-page illustration of the Devil. This portrait, grotesque and captivating, seems to reach out from the vellum, pulling those who gaze upon it into its malevolent grasp. It is said that this single image can drive a man to madness and that it can curse those who dare to lock eyes with its demonic visage. The manuscript is more than just a book; it is a relic imbued with the power of the infernal.

The legends surrounding its creation are equally macabre. As the story goes, the manuscript was crafted by a monk who broke his sacred vows and was condemned to be walled up alive. In a desperate bid for salvation, he promised to create a book that would glorify the monastery forever, a work so grand it would contain all human knowledge. As midnight approached and his strength waned, he invoked the Devil, trading his soul for the infernal assistance needed to complete the manuscript in a single night. Thus, the Codex Gigas was born, a product of dark pacts and desperate faith.

I knew that my own work must pay homage to this formidable artefact. In fact, the Codex Gigas is more than an artefact; it is a symbol of our eternal struggle with sin, temptation, and the forces that seek to corrupt us. In naming my book 'The Devil's Bible', I pay homage to this ancient manuscript and the terrifying power it represents. It is a reminder that evil is never far from us, lurking in the shadows, waiting for the moment to strike.

The Codex Gigas is more than an artefact; it is a symbol of our eternal struggle with sin, temptation, and the forces that seek to corrupt us. In naming my book 'The Devil's Bible', I pay homage to this ancient manuscript and the terrifying power it represents. It is a reminder that evil is never far from us, lurking in the shadows, waiting for the moment to strike. If you want to see this awe-inspiring book for yourself, it's on display at the National Library of Sweden in Stockholm.

In the pages of this book, my version of 'The Devil's Bible', I draw upon the shadow of the Codex Gigas. This is not merely a recounting of ancient lore but a journey into the heart of darkness, exploring the evil that men do and the demons that whisper in the night. Just as the Codex Gigas serves as a bridge between the sacred and the profane, my book aims to illuminate the darkness within us all.

In this book, I frequently use the term "Devil" almost as a placeholder, not specifically to refer to the Christian idea of the Devil, but rather to encompass the Devil from various religious traditions and personal interpretations. For instance, in Islamic theology, there is Iblis, the rebellious jinn who defied Allah. In Hinduism, there are malevolent beings like the asuras. In folklore across the globe, the Devil can take myriad forms, from the trickster spirits in African mythology to the cunning Yokai in Japanese beliefs. Moreover, individuals might have their own personal "Devils," embodying their deepest fears and darkest impulses. By using the term "Devil" in this broad, inclusive manner, we acknowledge the diverse and multifaceted nature of these malevolent entities.

Prepare to delve into forbidden knowledge, confront unspeakable horrors, and uncover secrets that have been hidden for centuries. 'The Devil's Bible' awaits, ready to reveal the true extent of the darkness that lies within. As you turn these pages, be ready to face the malevolent forces and ancient evils that have shaped our world from the shadows. The journey into the abyss begins now.

I invoke thee, Astaroth, from the West, great duke of Hell and keeper of secrets. Bestow upon me your profound knowledge and guide me in the ways of the arcane.

Foundations of Demonology

Demonology is not some innate supernatural ability or a gift bestowed at birth. From my perspective as a demonologist, it is the intense, often perilous study of demons and the beliefs surrounding them. Demons are typically considered to be supernatural beings that are malevolent in nature.

Traditionally, it's a branch of theology that delves into the classification of demons, their powers and activities, and their interactions with the human world. Far from being merely the stuff of horror films, demonology is a serious field of study for many scholars, religious practitioners, and paranormal investigators like myself.

Although demonology is not recognised as an academic field of study in the same way as disciplines like biology or physics, it remains a critical area of exploration for those of us deeply involved in the paranormal. It is not a subject you can study at university, and the demonologist title holds little credibility outside of dark circles.

However, if you devote yourself to the study and reach a profound understanding of demons and their malevolent ways, you will earn the right to be called a demonologist. By immersing yourself in demonology, you will, by the very essence of the title, become a guardian of forbidden knowledge.

Those of us who call ourselves demonologists have studied religious texts, historical accounts, and paranormal phenomena related to demons. This arms us with enough knowledge on the subject to be accepted as credible demonologists.

The study of demons stretches back through the dark corridors of history, embedded in the religious and cultural mythologies of countless ancient civilisations, where belief in malevolent spirits was common. In ancient Mesopotamia, Egypt, and Greece, people believed that demons could cause diseases and misfortune. These beliefs were often tied to religious practices, where rituals were performed to appease or ward off these harmful entities.

In the Christian tradition, demonology became more defined during the medieval period. The Church played a significant role in shaping the understanding of demons, often linking them to the Devil and the concept of evil. The infamous witch hunts and trials during the Middle Ages were partly fuelled by beliefs in demonic possession and influence.

It's for this reason that many think the study of demonology requires a foundation of religious belief. However, with similar malevolent entities appearing across various religions and cultures, it becomes clear that demons are more than mere antagonists in one religion's narrative.

This realisation means that in this book, we can peel away some of these ancient, conflicting, and outdated concepts and instead focus on the modern-day demon and its impact during paranormal investigations. This means you don't need religious beliefs to study the nature, behaviour, and control of demons. Many atheist paranormal investigators and those who have suffered haunting experiences recount their terrifying encounters with demons, regardless of their disbelief in the religious aspects of demonology.

Besides, demons are notorious deceivers, often masquerading as other types of supernatural entities, making it impossible to determine which tradition's rituals might be effective. Should you employ Christian exorcisms or perhaps another religion's practices? This ambiguity raises the question: would a Christian exorcism be effective against an Islamic demon?

You might be deeply religious, you may not adhere to any religious beliefs, or you might follow your own unique spiritual path. These personal beliefs can be more potent for you than the rituals of a religion you don't subscribe to. Attaching demons to specific religions is a treacherous endeavour, illustrating why traditional demonology can seem outdated for today's paranormal investigators.

This book, while steeped in the rich traditions of demonology, is not confined to the strictures of religious texts and doctrines. The approach to modern demonology outlined in 'The Devil's Bible' seeks to illuminate the shadowy corners where demons dwell, offering readers a guide to recognising and confronting the infernal in their own ghost-hunting endeavours. The infernal realm, as explored within these pages, intersects with the practice of ghost hunting in ways both profound and terrifying, transcending the boundaries of faith and culture.

Once you have absorbed the knowledge contained in this book, there are several ways you can utilise your newfound expertise. You may seek to diagnose, understand, or end the strange phenomena occurring in your own home. Alternatively, you might decide to help others with their demonic afflictions, using your skills to eradicate their torment. In such cases, you will need not only a deep understanding of demons but also respect, patience, and analytical thinking to validate and diagnose your clients' claims.

For paranormal investigators who focus on cases involving alleged demonic activity, demonology provides a framework for identifying phenomena commonly linked to demonic activity, such as foul smells, physical attacks, and other sinister or threatening behaviour.

A demonologist may offer help by ridding a location or object of a demonic attachment, or they may need to tackle a possession. This is one of the best-known aspects of demonology, where a demon inhabits a human body. To combat demonic possession, various religious traditions have rituals called exorcisms. An exorcism is a practice aimed at expelling the demon from the possessed person. These rituals can be elaborate, involving prayers, holy water, and religious symbols.

Knowledge of demons is one thing, but if you're going to start helping people afflicted by attachments or possessions, then you're going to need to develop and adhere to ethical guidelines in your practice to ensure that you work ethically with clients who believe they are experiencing a demonic haunting. These individuals are often vulnerable and may be dealing with complex psychological, emotional, or social issues.

Many people who believe they are experiencing demonic activity may actually be suffering from mental health conditions such as psychosis, anxiety, or depression. Ethical demonologists should prioritise the mental health needs of their clients and consider involving mental health professionals when necessary.

Gaining knowledge in psychology to differentiate between potential psychological disorders and genuine cases of demonic activity can help with this.

Conducting exorcisms or other rituals without proper training and understanding can be harmful. Misdiagnosing mental health issues as demonic possession can prevent individuals from receiving the medical care they need, leading to prolonged suffering or worsening conditions.

While anyone can technically call themselves a demonologist, doing so responsibly requires a commitment to genuine study and an understanding of the ethical implications involved. It carries with it a duty of care that should not be taken lightly. By being aware of the risks and taking steps to mitigate them, individuals can approach the study and investigation of demons more responsibly and safely.

The third, and most controversial, application of demonology is within ghost hunting or paranormal investigations. This often involves summoning or provoking demons to observe and understand their powers. Even without direct summoning, demons frequently make their presence known through Ouija boards or are blamed for various hauntings.

The haunted locations of today—abandoned asylums, derelict homes, and shadow-filled forests—serve as the battlegrounds where the infernal meets the corporeal. These are places where the veil between worlds is thinnest, where the lingering spirits of the dead and the predatory demons of the abyss converge, and where demonologists seek to come a step closer to evil.

Summoning demons requires continuous research and practice, often involving the recitation of arcane passages and incantations. These rituals are far more effective when performed with confidence and a deep understanding of their meanings, rather than stumbling through them. Memorising these invocations allows for a more natural and potent delivery, with confidence and belief amplifying their power.

As a demonologist, the tools I rely on in my relentless pursuit of understanding and combating demons are both diverse and deeply symbolic. Demonologists often arm themselves with tools that are not merely instruments of our trade but extensions of our intent and will, honed over centuries of confronting the darkest forces. These tools are steeped in tradition, each holding a unique power to repel, contain, or communicate with the malevolent entities that walk the shadows of our world.

First and foremost for me is my personal book of incantations, a tome filled with ancient rites, protective prayers, and powerful banishments. This book, weathered and worn, is my constant companion. Its pages, inscribed with the knowledge passed down through generations, are my most trusted ally. The words contained within are not mere ink on parchment, they are the distilled essence of centuries of wisdom and struggle against the infernal. Every line has been meticulously chosen for its power to invoke the divine and repel the damned.

Yet, 'The Devil's Bible' is not merely a reprint of this treasured manuscript. It is vital to understand that when dealing with demons, the true power lies not in the words themselves but in the intent behind them. Each individual's journey into the arcane is deeply personal, shaped by unique beliefs and experiences. The efficacy of an incantation depends on the practitioner's conviction and the alignment of the words with their own spiritual essence.

'The Devil's Bible' serves as a guide, offering a foundation of rituals and protections drawn from my own experiences. However, it is not a one-size-fits-all solution. You must choose words that resonate with your own beliefs and imbue them with your intent. The strength of your incantations comes from the deep personal meaning they hold for you. Trust in your own meaningful words, and the power they wield will be unmatched. Remember, it is your belief that gives these words their true potency, and with strong intent, you can command the darkness to retreat.

Then there is my crucifix, not just a symbol of faith but a weapon against the darkness. My decorative crucifix, ornate yet formidable, is always at hand. When faced with a demonic entity, it serves as a beacon of divine light, a reminder of the higher power that stands against the forces of evil. My crucifix is more than an emblem, it is an anchor that grounds me, its very sight and touch a torment to the malevolent spirits that seek to do harm.

My ceremonial skull, another vital tool, is steeped in mystery and ancient power. This skull, often misunderstood by the uninitiated, represents the bridge between life and death, the corporeal and the spiritual. It serves as a focal point during rituals, helping to channel energy and intent. The skull's hollow gaze reminds both the practitioner and the demon of the inexorable march of time and the inevitability of divine justice. It is a stark symbol that commands respect and instills fear in the hearts of the wicked.

My silver chalice, intricately engraved and consecrated, holds a dual purpose. It is used in rituals to contain holy water or sanctified wine, substances imbued with purifying properties. The act of drinking from the chalice or sprinkling its contents is a powerful gesture of sanctification and protection. Silver, with its intrinsic purity and ancient associations with the moon and divine feminine, adds an extra layer of potency. When I hold my chalice, I feel a connection to the myriad exorcists and demonologists who have wielded similar vessels in their sacred rites.

These tools—my crucifix, my ceremonial skull, my silver chalice—are deeply personal to me. They resonate with my beliefs and experiences, empowering me to confront the malevolent with unwavering resolve. However, it is important to recognise that each demonologist must find their own meaningful objects. The true strength of any tool lies in its connection to the practitioner's intent and beliefs. What works for one may not work for another, for it is the conviction and personal significance imbued in these items that make them powerful.

Beyond these personal tools, a demonologist's toolkit often includes a variety of other objects. Salt, known for its purifying properties, is used to create protective barriers and circles. Iron, especially in the form of nails or rods, is another traditional element known to repel malevolent entities. Its presence disrupts the energies that demons thrive on, creating a hostile environment for them.

Candles, especially black and white, are essential in rituals. Black candles absorb negative energy, while white candles invoke purity and protection. The light from these candles, flickering in the darkness, serves as a beacon of hope and a reminder of the light that will ultimately banish the shadows.

Incense, particularly frankincense and myrrh, is burned to purify spaces and summon protective spirits. The smoke, rising and curling through the air, carries prayers and incantations to the heavens, creating a sanctified space that demons find inhospitable.

Lastly, the demonologist's attire is chosen with care, often including robes or garments that symbolise protection and authority. These garments, sometimes adorned with protective symbols, help the practitioner maintain a focused and reverent state of mind, which is crucial for the successful execution of rituals.

My outfit is chosen to reflect both my seriousness in the field and the dark, enigmatic nature of my work. I am often clad in black, adorned with subtle yet significant markings—a cross here, an arcane symbol there—each one a ward against malevolent forces. The deep black hue absorbs the light, much like the mysteries I delve into, and serves as a stark reminder of the darkness I combat.

Every detail of my appearance is crafted to inspire both respect and a touch of fear, a reminder that I walk the fine line between this world and the next, unafraid and unyielding. Fans of 'Most Haunted' love my unique look. Every time I do an event, they want to have their picture taken with me.

My attire is not merely for show, it is a source of strength and protection. The carefully chosen garments and symbols I wear instil in me a profound sense of purpose and authority. This attire transforms me into a guardian against the darkness, bolstering my resolve and reminding me of my role as a beacon of light. It is this combination of belief in my tools and empowerment from my attire that fortifies my spirit, enabling me to confront and combat the infernal with unwavering confidence and determination.

By the salt and the flame, by the iron and the stone, I command you, spirit of darkness, to leave this object. You have no place here. I cast you out and bind you to the void.

The Devil's Dominion

Defining "demons" is a complex task due to their deep-rooted history in numerous cultures and religions. The concept of demons transcends time and geography, appearing in the beliefs of ancient Egyptians, Zoroastrians, and other ancient civilisations. The term itself originates from the Greek word "daemon," which does not inherently carry a negative connotation. In Greek mythology, a daemon could refer to a god, goddess, or any other entity higher than man but lower than God, essentially representing divine power.

However, in contemporary usage, "demon" has acquired a predominantly negative meaning, referring to evil, supernatural entities rooted in ancient religious texts and folklore. Unlike ghosts, which are typically considered to be the spirits of deceased humans, demons are non-human entities that have existed for centuries and have never lived.

Christian theology describes demons as fallen angels—beings who were once part of the heavenly host but were cast out due to their rebellion against divine authority. This rebellion imbued them with a deep-seated hatred for all that is good and holy, driving them to corrupt and destroy the fabric of the mortal world. They are often portrayed as tempters and deceivers, masters of illusion who prey on the weaknesses and fears of humans.

Another belief is that demons are the corrupted souls of the wicked dead. These spirits, having committed grievous sins in life, are transformed into malevolent entities in their next lives.

Other traditions have their own interpretations. They are often categorised based on their attributes and behaviours. A section of the 17th-century grimoire 'The Lesser Key of Solomon' lists 72 demons, each with a name, hierarchy, and specific powers.

At the top of this hierarchy is often a supreme ruler, such as Satan or Lucifer in Christian tradition, who commands legions of lesser demons. These demons are responsible for carrying out the punishments of the damned and perpetuating evil in the mortal world.

The ancient Hebrews had concepts of both friendly and unfriendly demons. They believed in some demons that were harmless and others that were more sinister and linked to negative aspects of mystical practices. This idea of classifying demons as either harmful or benign is found in many other religions, such as Hinduism and Zoroastrianism.

Demons are not mere relics of archaic scripture, they are entities that have evolved with the times, adapting their malevolent tactics to the modern world. Their influence can be seen not just through the lens of religious lore but also through the myriad encounters reported by ghost hunters, paranormal investigators, and ordinary individuals who have come face to face with the inexplicable.

Demons possess abilities that go beyond human capabilities, such as shape-shifting, which allows them to take on various guises to manipulate and terrorise their victims. They might appear as monstrous entities with horns, claws, and other grotesque features, or they might adopt more subtle, seductive forms to gain the trust and obedience of those they seek to corrupt. Their appearance is often tailored to evoke the deepest fears of those who behold them, making each encounter uniquely horrifying.

Demonic hauntings often begin subtly, almost imperceptibly, like a whispered curse carried on a chill breeze. Unseen eyes seem to watch from the corners of rooms, the hairs on the back of your neck prickling as the air grows thick with an unseen dread. These disturbances begin to escalate, perhaps to objects moving of their own accord, sliding across tables, or toppling from shelves in defiance of natural laws. Then from gentle nudges to violent thrusts, as if the demon grows bolder with each act of defilement.

Sudden, inexplicable cold spots manifest, sucking warmth and life from the room, leaving only a biting chill that seeps into the bones. The smell of sulphur, acrid and pungent, often accompanies these icy intrusions, a telltale sign of demonic presence. Electronics malfunction, lights flicker and die, and devices turn on and off as if commanded by an unseen hand, their normalcy perverted by a force beyond comprehension.

These entities are adept at influencing the mind and spirit and are capable of inducing hallucinations, instilling irrational fears, and manipulating emotions to drive their victims to despair and madness. Sleep can become a battlefield, with nightmares plaguing the minds of their victims and vivid and horrifying visions that linger long after waking. The demon's presence may culminate in physical attacks, invisible claws raking across skin, bruises and scratches appearing without cause, a tangible reminder of the unseen assailant.

Demons draw their power from the suffering and negative energies they create. They thrive in environments tainted by sin, despair, and corruption, using these energies to strengthen their hold on our world. Rituals, curses, and summoning acts can attract these entities, providing them with a foothold to wreak havoc.

Beyond their destructive capabilities, demons are often credited with vast, forbidden knowledge. They are said to possess insights into the darkest corners of reality, knowledge that can tempt those who seek power at any cost. However, this knowledge comes at a terrible price, often leading to the ultimate corruption or destruction of the seeker.

These beings are embodiments of pure evil, chaos, and darkness. Their sole purpose is to inflict suffering on the living. Some traditions even suggest that demons originate from realms beyond our own, perhaps from a previous universe or a parallel dimension. This otherworldly origin is often referred to as the "infernal realm."

The infernal realm, often referred to as Hell in many religious and mythological traditions, is a place of torment and darkness, traditionally considered the abode of demons and damned souls. This realm is characterised by its association with evil, suffering, and eternal punishment. It is widely believed to be the origin or dwelling place of demons, who serve as its denizens and agents of malevolence.

Imagery of the infernal realm often includes elements of darkness and fire. It is portrayed as a vast, shadowy abyss filled with unquenchable flames that cause immense pain without consuming the flesh. This paradoxical combination of fire and darkness symbolises the endless nature of the torment found there.

Demonologists often warn about various entities from the infernal realm beyond traditional demons. These entities are considered equally dangerous and malevolent, each with its own unique characteristics and threats, such as hellhounds. These supernatural dogs are known for their ferocity and association with death. They are often depicted with glowing red eyes and black fur, capable of immense strength and speed. Hellhounds are believed to serve as guardians of the underworld or as hunters for lost souls.

As someone with an interest in the paranormal, you've most likely come across the term "elementals," perhaps in connection with a famous haunting like that of Ireland's Leap Castle, or maybe you've encountered what you believe to be an elemental as part of a paranormal investigation. Elementals are non-human entities believed to be intimately connected with the forces of nature and the four classical elements: earth, water, air, and fire. Rooted in the works of Renaissance occultists such as Paracelsus, elementals include gnomes, undines, sylphs, and salamanders. While often seen as guardians of nature, they can be both benign and malevolent, influencing the natural world and occasionally interacting with humans.

Imps are small, mischievous creatures from the infernal realm. Although smaller and less powerful than demons, they still pose significant threats due to their mischievous and malevolent nature. Despite their diminutive size, imps can be quite dangerous, especially when they work in groups or are directed by more powerful demons.

Goblins are another class of small, malevolent creatures often associated with the infernal realm. They are known for their cunning and their ability to blend into the dark, shadowy places of the world. Another well-known infernal being is the gremlin. Popularised in modern folklore, gremlins are mischievous creatures known for sabotaging machinery and technology, especially onboard planes during World War II.

In Greco-Roman mythology, the Furies (or Erinyes) are deities of vengeance who reside in the infernal realm. They pursue and punish those who have committed heinous crimes, especially familial murders. While not demons in the traditional sense, their relentless pursuit and infliction of torment place them within the scope of infernal entities.

Originating from Native American folklore, the Wendigo is a malevolent spirit associated with cannibalism and insatiable hunger. It is believed to possess humans, driving them to commit acts of cannibalism. Wendigos are considered to be a type of demon or spirit that originates from the infernal realm, embodying the darkest aspects of human nature.

While imps and other similar entities may seem less intimidating compared to more powerful demons, their capacity for mischief, chaos, and harm should not be underestimated. These beings, often overlooked, can cause significant disruption and distress, especially when they act under the influence or command of greater demonic forces.

Demons are the insidious architects of humankind's suffering, lurking unseen behind physical and mental illness, bad luck, pain, and despair. These entities possess a power far surpassing that of human spirits, whether in life or death. Among their terrifying abilities are telepathy and telekinesis, tools they wield with malevolent intent to torment their victims.

With telepathy, demons pry into the darkest corners of a victim's mind, uncovering fears and worries to exploit. Their telekinetic powers, coupled with their inherent evil and violent nature, enable them to move objects, scratch, push, or even strike those they seek to dominate.

In whatever guise a demon appears, its ultimate goal remains constant: to erode the victim's free will, weaken them, and ultimately possess and control them. Demons are not limited to human hosts, they can attach themselves to objects, frequently choosing dolls and children's toys to instil terror.

Demonic hauntings can erupt anywhere and at any time, often beginning subtly and without immediate menace. These hauntings mimic the activities of other non-demonic disturbances: unexplained knocks and bangs, interference with electrical devices, and disembodied voices or whispers. But as a demon feeds on the victim's fear, depression, and sadness, the paranormal activity escalates. Nightmares become frequent, loud noises and growls pierce the night, foul odours permeate the air, and physical attacks become commonplace. Demons, cunning as they are, typically avoid manifesting early in a haunting, concealing their true nature until their grip on the victim is unshakeable, at which point full apparitions may be witnessed.

One of the most chilling phenomena related to demonic hauntings is materialisation. Demons can conjure substances from thin air, producing mysterious liquids that ooze from walls, flow from taps, or pool on the floor. These substances vary, from simple water to dark, tar-like fluids and even blood. Conversely, demons can also cause objects to dematerialise, only to have them reappear elsewhere or at a later time. The levitation of objects and the precise, deliberate breaking of items further signify a demon's presence, revealing an intelligence behind the damage that cannot be dismissed as mere accident.

Deception is a demon's forte. They weave lies with truths to bewilder their victims, often pretending to retreat only to strike when their prey is most vulnerable. They deceive by adopting angelic forms or mimicking the appearance and characteristics of children, exploiting the trust and sympathy of their victims.

Their primary goal is to erode the will and soul. This is the most feared ability attributed to demons is possession—the act of taking control of a person's body and mind, leading to erratic and harmful behaviour. Possession can be complete or partial, sometimes manifesting as a dual existence where the demon battles the host for dominance.

The tapestry of folklore is rich with tales of demons, their nefarious deeds, and the brave souls who dared to confront them. These stories, passed down through generations, offer glimpses into the myriad ways demons have been perceived across cultures and epochs. Here are a few particularly intriguing examples:

In Jewish folklore, the Dybbuk is a malicious spirit, often believed to be the soul of a dead person, that refuses to move on. This demon seeks to possess the living, usually to complete unfinished business or to exact revenge. One of the most famous tales involves a young bride who, on her wedding day, begins to act strangely and speak in a man's voice. A rabbi is called upon to exorcise the Dybbuk, revealing that the spirit belonged to a spurned lover who had died heartbroken. The rabbi successfully expels the Dybbuk, freeing the bride from its malevolent grasp.

Asmodeus, a demon from Persian and Judeo-Christian lore, is often associated with lust and wrath. In the Book of Tobit, part of the Apocrypha, Asmodeus falls in love with Sarah, a young woman, and kills seven of her husbands on their wedding nights out of jealousy. The hero, Tobias, is able to overcome Asmodeus with the help of the archangel Raphael. Tobias burns the liver and heart of a fish given to him by Raphael, producing a smoke that drives Asmodeus away to the remote parts of Egypt, thus allowing Tobias to marry Sarah unharmed.

Oni are fearsome demons in Japanese folklore, often depicted as hulking figures with red or blue skin, wild hair, and sharp horns. They are known for their immense strength and penchant for violence. One famous tale is the story of Shuten Dōji, an Oni who kidnapped and devoured young women from the capital city. A group of samurai, led by the hero Minamoto no Raikō, disguise themselves as monks to infiltrate Shuten Dōji's lair. They offer him poisoned sake, making him drunk and vulnerable. In his stupor, Shuten Dōji reveals his true form, but the samurai are able to behead him, thus ending his reign of terror.

Rakshasas are shape-shifting demons in Hindu and Buddhist mythology, often depicted with grotesque features and a taste for human flesh. One of the most famous Rakshasas is Ravana, the ten-headed king of Lanka, who kidnaps Sita, the wife of Lord Rama. The epic Ramayana details Rama's quest to rescue Sita, involving battles with numerous demons. Ravana, despite his formidable powers and intellect, is ultimately slain by Rama, symbolising the triumph of good over evil.

These tales, filled with horror and heroism, illustrate the deep-rooted fear and fascination humans have with demons. They serve as cautionary stories, reminding us of the ever-present dangers lurking in the shadows and the strength required to confront them.

By the shadows that dwell in the depths of night,

By the spirits that crave eternal blight,

I call upon the forces dark and deep,

To awaken from their deathless sleep.

Identifying the Infernal

Throughout my extensive career as a demonologist and paranormal investigator, I have encountered numerous instances of malevolent forces that defy conventional explanations. Confirming they are the work of a demonic presence is not as easy as one might think. It is a skill requiring a blend of keen observation, deep understanding, and an unwavering resolve.

People often perceive demons as inherently evil, controlling, and menacing. The problem arises in trying to distinguish between a demon and a malignant human spirit. Just as there are both good and bad humans, there must be evil ghosts as well as benign ones.

Many demonology texts are filled with exhaustive lists of demons, their traits, and religious origins. I do not trust these lists, nor do I use them. Demons are master deceivers, lying about their identities, making it impossible to know if these lists are accurate. How can anyone be certain they are truly dealing with one of the listed entities? Relying on these lists can lead to dangerous misconceptions and underestimations of the demonic threat. Instead, it is crucial to approach each encounter with a fresh perspective, relying on observation and direct evidence to discern the nature of these malevolent forces.

Through years of investigation, I have honed methods to identify the subtle yet significant differences between malevolent human spirits and demons. This chapter will guide you through the telltale signs of a demonic presence, helping you to discern the nature of the supernatural forces you might encounter.

Phantom knocks, disembodied voices, and the movement of objects are common examples. Some might explain these clues through natural environmental causes, others might attribute them to ghosts or poltergeists, and still others might label this activity as demonic. These signs of a supernatural entity interacting with the physical world tend to be subtle, especially in the early stages of a haunting. By the time it becomes clear you are dealing with a demon, it could be too late.

Demons are master manipulators, often presenting themselves at first as benign or even friendly spirits to gain the trust of their victims. They might mimic the voices and appearances of loved ones or create illusions to lull people into a false sense of security. Demons often focus specifically on one person, sometimes posing as a child, especially when the victim is a child. This may start as an imaginary friend. As their true nature gradually reveals itself, these deceptions turn into nightmares, eroding the victim's mental and emotional stability.

Distinguishing between demons, poltergeists, and malevolent human spirits is challenging due to overlapping characteristics. Each type of entity has its own distinct traits and behaviours, but many of their traits, such as moving objects, unusual sounds, and temperature changes, can appear similar, making any definitive conclusion about the nature of a haunting unlikely. However, there are some commonly believed factors and trends that can help an investigator diagnose a demonic haunting, some of which are unique to demons and some that aren't.

One symptom of demons is foul odours, such as sulphur or rotting flesh. These unpleasant smells are often reported in cases of demonic activity but are also common in poltergeist cases. Similarly, objects moving are reported in both demonic and poltergeist cases, as well as some cases involving human spirits. This can involve heavy furniture or other objects moving on their own, sometimes with great force. Doors may slam shut or open on their own, and furniture may be overturned. In many demonic cases, the objects do not merely move or disappear as with a poltergeist—they are hurled with violent intent, often aimed directly at the living.

Strange sounds are linked to many different types of hauntings. While loud bangs or screams might fit all hauntings, noises such as growls are often more commonly reported in cases of suspected demonic activity. However, the sometimes reported phenomenon of ghost animals could also explain these growls. Sudden and extreme temperature drops in specific areas, often referred to as "cold spots," are sometimes said to indicate a demonic presence, but this phenomenon also has strong links to human spirits. Specifically, a temperature drop is often said to be the first sign of a ghostly presence.

Perhaps the trait most closely linked specifically to demons is the experience of physical attacks. Victims may experience sudden and inexplicable bruises or burns on their bodies without any known cause, often in places they could not reach themselves. This behaviour ties neatly into the idea of what demons are: malevolent and evil. However, both demons and traditional hauntings involve physical phenomena such as moving objects. Therefore, both are capable of physically affecting a person, given malicious intent. We can't rule out that an evil ghost is responsible for a physical attack.

Harm specifically in the form of scratches and bites, however, is often more closely associated with demons, especially when the marks appear in threes. These marks are not random but are typically symbols or sigils, ancient and arcane, etched into the flesh by unseen claws. In demonic cases, individuals may experience more violent assaults, such as being pushed, slapped, or even thrown across a room.

Although I generally favour observational methods over strictly biblical descriptions, the religious significance of the number three persists. This is believed to mock the Holy Trinity, symbolising the demon's malevolent intent and contempt for sacred symbols.

The first sign of a demonic presence often manifests in the atmosphere itself. While a ghostly haunting might bring a chill to the air, a demon brings an oppressive heaviness, a tangible weight that presses down upon the chest and makes breathing laborious. It is as if the very air is tainted with malice, thick and cloying, sapping the vitality from all who dwell within its reach.

Fires may ignite spontaneously, and water may turn foul, reeking of sulphur and decay. These are not the playful tricks of a mischievous spirit but the calculated acts of an entity bent on harm. Another sign often believed to indicate a demonic presence is the appearance of unusual symbols or markings on walls, floors, or other surfaces. These often include inverted crosses, inverted pentagrams, or other occult symbols associated with dark rituals and malevolent forces.

One of the most telling signs of a demonic infestation is the behaviour of animals. Although this is also reported in non-demonic hauntings, when a demon is involved, the effects tend to be more pronounced. Dogs, in particular, are highly sensitive to these malevolent beings. They will growl, bark, and cower in the presence of a demon, their hackles raised and eyes wide with terror. Cats, too, will react, hissing and arching their backs, their fur standing on end. Even birds will flee the area, their natural instincts urging them to escape the unseen danger.

I often make contact with entities from the infernal realm during paranormal investigations. Those who dare to engage in such practices must navigate a labyrinth of potential deception and malevolence. Among the various methods used to reach out to these dark entities, some of the most common include the use of Ouija boards, automatic writing, scrying, Electronic Voice Phenomena (EVP), and the use of spirit boxes.

Ouija boards, with their seemingly innocent facade, have long been a gateway for those seeking to contact the spirit world. Participants place their hands on a planchette, which glides across the board to spell out messages. While often dismissed as a parlour game, the Ouija board can act as a conduit for demonic forces, manipulating the planchette to deliver cryptic and often disturbing messages. Demons can often be detected using a Ouija board through mischievous behaviour, inconsistent answers, or outright lies. Typically, when starting a session, you might call out to any spirits present with, "Is there anybody there?" If the planchette moves towards "yes," it indicates a spirit's presence, but if it moves to "no," this is often seen as a sign of a demonic entity. Additionally, asking the spirit its age and seeing the planchette point to zero is a strong indicator of demonic contact.

Similarly, automatic writing involves surrendering control of one's hand to allow a spirit to communicate through written words. This practice can yield messages that range from the mundane to the deeply unsettling, often revealing knowledge far beyond the scribe's own understanding.

Scrying, on the other hand, involves gazing into reflective surfaces like mirrors, crystal balls, or water to receive visions or messages from the other side. Demons can use these visions to convey their will, often cloaked in symbolism and shadow.

Although I'm not a strong advocate for the use of EVP, it is a method favoured by modern paranormal investigators. By recording ambient sounds and analysing the playback, investigators capture voices or messages that were not audible during the recording session. These disembodied voices can offer chilling evidence of a demonic presence, especially if the captured voice is gruff, deep, or animalistic. Demons can also be detected in EVPs through growling sounds.

Demons can also make their presence known through spirit boxes. These ghost-hunting devices rapidly scan through various radio frequencies, producing bursts of white noise and static. Within this noise, investigators listen for EVP-like spirit responses. Because this is a real-time method of communication, you can often obtain a great deal of information about the nature of the entity you are communicating with.

Demons do not simply haunt a location, they infest it, creating a long-term presence that can persist for years, even decades. These "attachments" can take hold of specific people, objects, or places. When a demon attaches itself to something, the result is a demonic haunting. Once an

attachment has been formed, a demon often attempts to make the environment safe for itself. This can result in the sudden, unexplained death of pets because pets can help to expose them. Protective or spiritual items may also be destroyed or go missing, including protective items like sentimental jewellery or good luck charms.

Demons excel at psychological warfare, targeting the fears, insecurities, and weaknesses of their victims. They induce vivid nightmares, paranoia, and hallucinations, driving individuals to the brink of madness. They may hear voices, guttural and mocking, whispering vile threats in their ears. In the waking hours, paranoia sets in, and the afflicted may become withdrawn, aggressive, or even violent, their minds slowly succumbing to the relentless assault. These psychological attacks are designed to isolate the victim and break down their will to resist, eventually leading to one of the most terrifying behaviours of demons, their ability to possess individuals. The possessed person's personality may change drastically, becoming hostile, aggressive, and unrecognisable to their loved ones.

During possession, the demon takes control of the victim's body, often exhibiting superhuman strength, speaking in unknown languages, or displaying knowledge of hidden or private matters. Genuine demonic communication may include accurate predictions of future events, the use of ancient or obscure languages, and the revelation of deeply personal information that the individual could not possibly know.

Confirming a demonic possession involves ruling out other explanations such as mental illness, delusion, or faked incidents. Once these are excluded, a genuine demonic possession may be considered. One method to confirm a demonic presence is to use a protective item without the victim's knowledge. This could be any object charged with positive energy or of religious significance, such as holy water. Hold the protective item behind the possessed person without their knowledge to see if they react. A true demonic entity will react to its proximity. Similarly, you can sprinkle both regular tap water and blessed water over the victim to see if there is a different reaction.

Signs of possession include the victim not blinking, withdrawing from family and friends, and losing interest in usual activities. They may become emotionally intense, particularly angry towards others. Look for unexplained marks on the body, such as scratches, bites, and bruises, in places the victim cannot reach. The possessed may show signs of illness and weakness, such as weight loss, hair loss, change in skin tone, loss of appetite, vomiting, and loss of energy. Conversely, they might display extreme strength beyond their normal capabilities.

In my years of battling these infernal beings, I have learned that the key to confirming a demonic presence lies in the details. You must observe and analyse every occurrence, no matter how trivial it may seem. Patterns will emerge, each piece of the puzzle fitting together to reveal the true nature of the entity at work.

With this light, I seal your departure. With this darkness, I reclaim my peace.

Diabolical Diary

As a demonologist, there are several events in the demonic year that are particularly powerful. Each year, the cycle of the seasons is mirrored by a cycle of supernatural activity. There are times when the veil between our world and the realms beyond grows thin, when the energies of the cosmos align to create windows of heightened spiritual and demonic presence.

Spring Equinox

The demonic year begins with the Spring Equinox, a time of renewal and balance, but also a period when dark forces may seek to disrupt the harmony of the reborn Earth. The March equinox, also known as the vernal equinox, marks the first day of spring in the Northern Hemisphere. This period is the origin of the modern-day festival of Easter, which began as a celebration of the renewed cycle of life and fertility, often accompanied by sexual rituals.

This time signifies the awakening of all nature from the winter season, initiating the cycle of renewed life—symbolised today by eggs and young hopping bunnies. Pagans originally celebrated this time of renewal by invoking Ēostre or Ostara, the Goddess of Spring, dawn, and fertility. Fertility was of immense significance to ancient civilisations due to its importance for the survival of the species.

Festivals were held to honour the Goddess Ēostre, celebrating rebirth and ensuring future generations. These festivities likely included erotic rituals and even group sex acts. As Christianity spread across the globe, thanks to the Roman Empire around 312 AD, many pagan rituals, including the celebration of the Spring Equinox, were adopted. Emperor Constantine I recognised that incorporating pagan rituals into Christian practices would ease the Romans' transition to Christianity, as many Romans identified as pagans and were reluctant to abandon their traditions. This is how the traditional celebration of Ēostre and the Spring Equinox was co-opted by early Christians and transformed into the modern-day celebration of Easter, incorporating the story of Christ's resurrection into the symbolism.

Beltane

Later in the spring comes May Day, also known as Beltane, one of the four great witches' sabbaths, and a day marked by maypole dancing. Thought to be the oldest British festival, May Day falls on May 1 and was celebrated by Druids around 2,000 years ago.

Beltane marks the midpoint of spring, situated halfway between the Spring Equinox and the Summer Solstice. At this time of year, the energy shifts noticeably from the beginning of the season. The days are longer, the sun sets later, and the warmth begins to embrace the Earth. The name "Beltane" derives from the Gaelic word meaning "bright fire." It was a fire festival celebrating the onset of summer. The ancient Celts used Beltane to mark the changing seasons, often recognising only two main periods: summer, starting with Beltane, and winter, beginning with Samhain on October 31.

The Beltane rituals were essential for the protection of the Gaelic Celts' herds. Enormous bonfires were lit, believed to possess protective powers. Herdsmen drove their animals through the smoke, while people took embers home to ignite their hearth fires, ensuring protection for the months ahead.

Beltane, like Samhain, is a time when the veil between worlds is thin. However, while Samhain is about connecting with the spirits of the dead, Beltane is when the veil between the human world and the realm of faeries and nature spirits grows thin. These entities are especially active during Beltane. Offerings were left out for the faeries and in other sacred places to appease these spirits, ensuring a successful growing season.

It is said that witches would ride their he-goats or broomsticks to mystical ancient places in the early hours of May Day, where they would make sacrifices to the Devil himself. Thankfully, sacrifice is no longer practiced, but many ancient May Day traditions, including maypole dancing, persist in Britain. Couples would dance around the maypole—a giant phallic symbol in the middle of the village green—after returning from the fields following a night of lovemaking.

Beltane was also a time for grand meetings, celebrations, and feasting. In ancient times, it was difficult for large groups to gather during the cold winter months due to the lack of suitable spaces. Beltane provided one of the first opportunities for people to come together after the harsh winter. Traditional Beltane celebrations had largely faded by the mid-twentieth century. However, these traditions saw a revival with the rise of the modern Wiccan movement. Wicca, founded in the early twentieth century, draws from a patchwork of beliefs and celebrations from various Earth-based cultures across Europe. While it uses the ancient Gaelic name "Beltane" for its mid-spring celebration, many of its practices actually stem from ancient German and Roman fertility festivals.

For Wiccans and neo-Pagans, Beltane is a time to honour nature's incredibly fertile energy. Nature's ability to reproduce itself in such a stunning and wondrous way is celebrated. This is a time to honour the power of fertility in all life forms. In our modern culture, sex is often viewed with shame and immorality, something to be hidden away. Beltane is a time to reclaim and reconnect with your own sexual energy—not just for the power of creating new life, but for the sheer pleasure it brings. Sex is a sacred and integral part of life, offering the opportunity to experience deep, transcendent, overwhelming pleasure.

Summer Solstice

The Summer Solstice, falling on June 21, marks the longest day and the shortest night of the year. This day is a turning point, a moment when the sun reaches its zenith and the Earth is bathed in its fullest light. Yet, within this brilliance lies a hidden darkness, for the solstice is also a time of great power and potential peril.

Ancient cultures around the world have revered the Summer Solstice, recognising its significance in the eternal dance of light and dark. For the Celts, this was Litha, a festival celebrating the power of the sun. Bonfires were lit to honour the solar deity, and people would jump through the flames to purify and protect themselves from malevolent forces. But the Summer Solstice is not just a time of celebration. It is also a period when the veil between worlds is thin, similar to Beltane and Samhain. This thinning allows for increased interaction between our world and the realms beyond. Spirits, faeries, and other supernatural entities are believed to be more active, their influence more potent.

For demonologists, the solstice is a double-edged sword. While it is a time of immense natural energy, this energy can be harnessed for both good and ill. Demons and other malevolent beings may seek to exploit this power, using it to strengthen their hold on the human world. Rituals of protection are crucial during this time, as is vigilance against the dark forces that may seek to disrupt the balance. The solstice's connection to fertility and growth also carries a darker undertone. Ancient rites often included offerings and sacrifices to ensure the continued blessing of the land. These practices, steeped in blood and fire, remind us of the thin line between life and death, creation and destruction.

In modern times, the Summer Solstice continues to be celebrated by Wiccans, Pagans, and those who honour the old ways. These celebrations often include gatherings at sacred sites, where participants dance, sing, and perform rituals to harness the solstice's energy. However, the echoes of ancient fears remain. The solstice is a time to revel in the sun's power but also to respect the shadows that linger at the edges of its light.

As we embrace the light of the longest day, we must also be mindful of the darkness it can reveal. The

Summer Solstice is a time of balance, a reminder that with great power comes great responsibility. It is a moment to celebrate the sun's triumph over darkness, even as we prepare for the inevitable return of the night.

Samhain

Samhain, known today as Halloween, holds a special place in the hearts of ghost hunters and those fascinated by the supernatural. As a demonologist, I have always been drawn to the profound significance of this ancient festival. The ancient Celts saw Samhain as a deeply spiritual time. October 31 lies exactly between the autumn equinox and the winter solstice. This unique positioning made it a period when the veil between the worlds of the living and the dead was said to be at its thinnest, allowing for easier communication with the spirits of the deceased. It is during this time that the boundaries between the physical world and the spirit world blur, creating an atmosphere ripe for supernatural encounters.

Celtic people considered Samhain their New Year, marking the death of the old year and the birth of the new. This period was not merely symbolic but was believed to possess genuine spiritual significance, providing a unique opportunity to connect with the other side. Bonfires were lit to guide the souls of the dead and to ward off malevolent spirits. The flames and smoke were believed to have protective qualities, ensuring the safety of the living during this vulnerable time.

Although the name Samhain has been somewhat lost to time, many of its ancient traditions have endured. One of the most recognisable is the practice of dressing in costumes. By disguising themselves as ghosts, monsters, and demons, people believed they could blend in with any spirits crossing over while the veil was thin, thus protecting themselves from malevolent entities. This practice has evolved into the Halloween costumes we see today, but its roots are deeply entwined with the desire to protect oneself from the unseen.

So, why did Samhain slip from our calendars? Around the eighth century, like several other Pagan festivals, it was adopted by the Christian Church. Positioned strategically the day before All Saints Day, also known as All Hallows Day, it became known as All Hallows Eve, eventually morphing into what we now know as Halloween. This was a smart, cunning move by the Christian Church. By incorporating existing Pagan festivals into the Christian calendar, they facilitated the transition of believers to the new religion without forcing them to abandon their cherished traditions and practices. This blending of customs allowed for a smoother cultural and religious shift, ensuring that many of the old ways continued to influence modern practices.

Modern Halloween retains much of the dark, mysterious allure of Samhain. The traditions of carving pumpkins, originally turnips, into grotesque faces and lighting them from within harken back to the old Celtic practice of creating lanterns to ward off evil spirits. Trick-or-treating has roots in the ancient custom of leaving offerings to appease wandering spirits.

As we celebrate Halloween today, it is fascinating to consider its ancient roots in Samhain. This festival of the dead continues to captivate us, a testament to its enduring power and the thin veil between our world and the unknown. The darkness of Samhain is a reminder of the ever-present shadows that lurk just beyond our understanding, waiting for the moment when the veil once again grows thin.

Winter Solstice

The Winter Solstice, occurring on December 21, marks the longest night and the shortest day of the year. This time of deep darkness is a pivotal moment in the wheel of the year, a period shrouded in mystery and potent with ancient power. As a demonologist, I have always found the Winter Solstice to be particularly significant.

This is the night when darkness reigns supreme, a time when the forces of the night are at their most powerful. It is a moment when the barriers between our world and the shadowy realms are at their thinnest, making it a prime opportunity for demonic activity and other supernatural occurrences.

Ancient cultures around the world have long recognised the significance of the Winter Solstice. For the Celts, this was the festival of Yule, a time to honour the rebirth of the sun. Bonfires were lit to chase away the darkness, and evergreens were brought into the home as symbols of life enduring through the harshest of times. But beneath these festive traditions lay a deep respect for the darker aspects of the solstice.

The Winter Solstice is not merely a time of celebration; it is also a time of great caution. The long hours of night provide ample opportunity for malevolent entities to roam freely. In many traditions, this is a time when spirits, ghosts, and demons are particularly active. It is said that during these long nights, the gates to the underworld are open wide, allowing these entities to cross into our realm with greater ease.

In my own experience, the Winter Solstice is a time when one must be especially vigilant. Rituals of protection are paramount. One must guard against the encroaching darkness with light and purity. It is a time to strengthen one's defences, to cleanse the home and spirit of any lurking malevolence. The use of candles, blessed by ritual, and the burning of protective herbs such as sage and juniper can help to ward off unwanted spirits.

The solstice also holds a mirror to our inner darkness. It is a time for introspection, for confronting the shadows within ourselves. Just as the sun is reborn after the longest night, we too have the opportunity to emerge from our own periods of darkness, renewed and strengthened. This is the true power of the Winter Solstice—the ability to face and transcend the darkness, both external and internal.

Modern celebrations of the Winter Solstice often overlook these darker aspects, focusing instead on the return of the light. However, for those of us who work closely with the supernatural, the solstice remains a time of profound significance. It is a reminder that light and dark are inextricably linked and that one cannot exist without the other. The Winter Solstice teaches us to respect the darkness, understand its place in the natural order, and harness its power wisely.

As we gather to mark the longest night, let us not forget the ancient wisdom that accompanies this time. Let us honour the darkness, prepare for its challenges, and embrace the returning light with renewed strength and clarity.

Blood Moons and Eclipses

Interspersed among these key points are the blood moons and eclipses that disrupt the natural order and create conditions ripe for demonic activity. These are times when the universe itself seems to breathe, when the unseen becomes seen, and the boundaries between worlds blur.

These celestial events are among the most awe-inspiring and ominous phenomena in the night sky. As a demonologist, I have always found these lunar events to be of particular interest, not just for their celestial beauty but for the heightened supernatural activity they seem to provoke.

A blood moon occurs during a total lunar eclipse when the Earth casts its shadow on the moon, giving it a deep, eerie red hue. This spectral transformation has long been associated with omens and portents of doom. Throughout history, blood moons have been viewed as harbingers of disaster, signalling times of great upheaval and change. In my own experience, these lunar events are indeed times when the veil between worlds grows thin, allowing for increased interaction with the supernatural.

Eclipses, both lunar and solar, are times when natural order is temporarily disrupted. The sun or moon, typically sources of consistent light and stability, are obscured, casting the world into an unusual state of darkness. This disruption creates an ideal environment for demonic activity. The shadows lengthen, and the boundaries between the seen and unseen blur.

During blood moons and eclipses, I have often encountered heightened paranormal phenomena. Some of my most compelling ghost hunts have taken place under these lunar events. The spirits seem more active, their presence more palpable. It is as if the cosmic disturbance stirs the very fabric of the supernatural, making it easier for entities to manifest and interact with our world.

On several occasions, my team and I have documented significant spikes in activity during these times. From disembodied voices and shadow figures to sudden drops in temperature and unexplained equipment malfunctions, the evidence collected during blood moons and eclipses is some of the most convincing I have encountered.

But these events are not without their danger. The increased activity means that malevolent entities are also more likely to be encountered. Rituals of protection are crucial. Before embarking on a ghost hunt during a blood moon or eclipse, we take extra precautions, performing cleansing rituals and arming ourselves with protective symbols and herbs. The use of salt, sage, and blessed objects becomes even more important to ensure our safety and the safety of those with us.

For those who seek to explore the supernatural, blood moons and eclipses offer unparalleled opportunities. However, they should be approached with respect and caution. These are times of great power and potential peril. The energy unleashed during these events can be harnessed for good or ill, and one must be prepared for both outcomes.

As we gaze up at the blood-red moon or watch the sun disappear behind the moon, let us remember the ancient wisdom that accompanies these phenomena. They are reminders of the delicate balance between light and dark, order and chaos. For those of us who walk the line between worlds, blood moons and eclipses are times to embrace the mystery and power of the universe while remaining ever vigilant against the shadows that lurk within.

By the purity of this water, I expel you, demon. Leave this vessel and return to the shadows from whence you came.

Deflecting Darkness

Interacting with demons is a perilous endeavour fraught with unseen dangers and dark forces eager to exploit any weakness. As we step into the abyss, it is crucial to fortify ourselves spiritually and mentally against the malevolent entities that lie in wait.

There are a few basic rules you should follow to go some way towards keeping you safe. Most importantly, under no circumstances should you ever utter a demon's name aloud unless you intend to summon it. If a demon reveals its name, speaking it gives the entity power, acting as an invitation to draw closer and grow stronger. Remember, demons are always watching, lurking in the unseen corners of our world.

Maintaining a positive outlook and avoiding fear and paranoia are critical, as fear can act as an entry point for demonic influence. Positive affirmations and a thorough understanding of demonic tactics help in maintaining a rational and composed mindset.

You should also avoid provoking or angering dark entities. Approach them with caution and respect. When asking questions, be polite and always thank them for their responses.

Never be alone with someone who is possessed. The dark energy consuming them can be contagious, dragging you into the abyss and leaving you susceptible to possession. Demons feed on fear and despair, and their malevolent influence can be overwhelming.

Demons can attach themselves to any object, often lying dormant until disturbed or transferred to a new owner. Never bring second-hand items into your home without first cleansing them. We will cover cleansing methods in detail later, exploring how to protect yourself and your environment from these malevolent forces.

Many demonologists carry protective items to defend against demonic influence. These talismans can be a lifeline in the darkest moments. Traditionally, demonologists would arm themselves with a crucifix, holy water, a Bible, or rosaries.

The crucifix, representing the crucifixion of Jesus Christ, is a powerful symbol in Christian demonology. It is believed to ward off evil spirits and protect against demonic attacks. Wearing a crucifix as a necklace, placing one above doorways, or carrying one as I do can serve as a constant shield against malevolent forces. I am always seen with my large trademark crucifix. This handheld cross has become my talisman, reflecting both my faith and my belief in its power to ward off evil.

Holy water is one of the most universally recognised protective items. Consecrated by religious clergy, it is used in rituals to bless and purify people, objects, and spaces. Holy books, such as the Bible, Quran, or other sacred texts, are powerful tools in protecting against demonic entities. Rosary beads, used in Catholic prayer, are considered a potent tool for protection and meditation. Carrying rosary beads or keeping them in the home can provide a spiritual barrier against demonic entities.

These items remain potent if they resonate with your faith. However, your talisman doesn't have to be of a religious nature. You can pick any item for spiritual protection or defence. It doesn't matter what the object is, as long as it is something you believe in strongly that holds specific significance to your beliefs. This belief charges the item with your positive energy, creating a powerful shield against malevolent forces. Many choose jewellery like bracelets, necklaces, or medallions. Protective symbols often featured in jewellery include the Celtic triple knot, known as a triquetra, or specific runic symbols.

Another common symbol is a pentacle, a five-pointed star enclosed in a circle that is used in Wiccan and Pagan traditions for protection and balance. Other symbols include the Eye of Horus, an ancient Egyptian symbol believed to provide protection and ward off evil; the Hamsa hand, popular in Middle Eastern cultures;

and the nazar. Often referred to as the evil eye, the nazar is a Middle Eastern talisman meant to ward off the evil eye—a curse believed to be cast by a malevolent glare, usually when the recipient is unaware.

Various medals are used in demonology for their protective qualities. The Saint Benedict Medal is particularly revered in Catholic tradition. It bears inscriptions and symbols believed to ward off evil and protect the wearer from harm. Similarly, the miraculous medal, associated with the Virgin Mary, is worn for divine protection.

If you're considering protective items, silver is a wise choice. Silver is said to purify its surroundings and disrupt spirit communication, as does iron. Iron, in particular, is thought to ward off evil spirits and demons. Hanging iron horseshoes above doorways or using iron nails in construction can provide protection.

Amulets of protection or charms made from natural substances, crystals, or semi-precious stones are also popular. There is a long-standing belief that crystals and certain stones can protect against demons, demonic hauntings, and possession. When choosing a stone, select one that appeals to you and focus your positive energy on it. Traditionally, stones like amber, black onyx, ruby, obsidian, amethyst, hematite, jade, and tourmaline are used. Peridot is said to ward off demons, and chrysoberyl is believed to specifically protect against possession. Iron is also reputed to repel demons; iron chains are said to be the only type of restraint that works on a demonic entity. Carrying these stones, placing them in living spaces, or wearing them as jewellery can help shield against demonic influence.

Salt is another frequently used protective item, believed to repel demons and other negative spirits. It can be worn in the form of rock crystals in a pouch around the neck, providing constant protection during paranormal investigations or séances. I often use salt, specifically sea salt, to draw a circle on the floor, creating a safe area that demons cannot penetrate. Salt has long been considered a purifying substance with protective qualities. In many cultures, it is used to create barriers against evil spirits. Sprinkling salt around the perimeter of a home, in doorways, or on windowsills is believed to prevent demonic entities from entering. Salt can also be dissolved in water and used to cleanse objects or spaces.

Another method to protect a house involves using a small terracotta bowl known as a demon bowl. These bowls, inscribed with incantations or religious texts according to your beliefs, are said to repel or trap demons. Traditionally, the bowls were buried in the foundations at each of the four corners of a house. In modern homes, they might be equally effective if placed in windows or entrance halls.

Bells and chimes are used in many cultures to dispel negative energies and summon protective spirits. The sound of ringing bells is believed to drive away demons and purify the environment. Hanging wind chimes or ringing bells in the home can create a protective atmosphere.

Cleansing rituals play a crucial role in maintaining an environment free of negative energies but can also be used to cleanse objects or people. The most common of these rituals involves the burning of sage, also known as smudging. Smudge sticks, pre-wrapped bundles of dried sage, are the most convenient form for smudging. These can be purchased online, at stores selling incense, or made from sage you grow yourself. The practice is rooted in Native American traditions but widely adopted for its cleansing properties. The smoke from burning sage is believed to purify spaces, objects, and individuals, driving away negative energies and malevolent entities. Similarly, incense, particularly frankincense and myrrh, is used in various religious rituals to sanctify and protect. Others use palo santo wood, cedar, sweetgrass, lavender, or other herbs.

The ritual of smudging is steeped in ancient ceremonial traditions, but it's crucial to adapt it in a way that resonates with you personally. Perform your ritual slowly, with full awareness, and in a mindful manner, dedicating at least 10 to 15 minutes to the process. Begin the ritual by focusing your energy, lighting the tip of the sage with a match, lighter, or candle, and gently waving it until it begins to smoulder.

If smudging yourself or another person, pass the smouldering smudge stick around the body, allowing the smoke to envelop the person from head to toe. Take your time, ensuring the smoke thoroughly surrounds them. This same procedure can be used to cleanse any object by moving the burning sage around it and engulfing it in smoke. For added protection, place the object on a piece of white cloth and sprinkle it with salt. Leave it in a safe, undisturbed place for several days.

When smudging a building or room, move around with the burning sage. Ensure at least one door or window is open to provide an exit route for the demon. Most people start at the front door or main entrance, moving consistently in one direction around the building, either clockwise or anti-clockwise, without neglecting smaller rooms like utility rooms, ensuite bathrooms, and garages. In each room, fill the entire space with sage smoke, letting it drift into all corners and dark spaces, as corners are said to accumulate stagnant energy. As you pass an open door or window, waft the smoke outside to carry the negative energies from your home. Once you have smudged all areas and returned to the starting point, extinguish your sage bundle by stubbing it out.

In the battle against demonic forces, these protective measures serve as our armour and shield, empowering us to confront the darkness with unwavering resolve. This is why I am never without a personal talisman of some kind during investigations, whether it's a necklace, my book, or a crucifix.

By our blood and by our union, we command thee. As our bodies merge, so too do our wills. Let our desire be manifest, our will be done.

Infernal Infestations

Demons cannot possess objects or places in the conventional sense, but they can certainly attach themselves to them through a sinister process known as infestation. This is when a demonic entity forms a persistent and often parasitic bond with an individual, object, or place.

Demons can attach themselves to individuals for various reasons, often targeting those who are emotionally vulnerable or have dabbled in occult practices. Personal attachments can severely impact the victim's life, relationships, and overall well-being.

Unlike full possession, where the demon takes direct control of a person's body and mind, an attachment involves a more subtle yet deeply invasive connection. This bond allows the demon to exert influence over the host, often causing physical, emotional, and psychological distress.

A common symptom of attachment is a sense of being drained or exhausted, both physically and emotionally. The host may struggle with sleep disturbances, recurring nightmares, and a general decline in health and vitality.

Individuals with attachments often report experiencing paranormal phenomena. This can include hearing disembodied voices, seeing shadowy figures, or feeling sudden, inexplicable chills. These experiences are often dismissed initially but can become more frequent and intense over time.

In some cases, demons attach themselves to specific objects, often those associated with dark history or occult rituals. Yet, their vile influence can extend to nearly any object, barring those imbued with strong protective properties. These objects can become conduits for the demon's influence, affecting anyone who comes into contact with them. Such objects may include antiques, jewellery, or even vehicles. They often favour items with faces, which is why cursed dolls are such a prevalent and disturbing manifestation.

A demonically infested item is not always active, lying in wait, dormant, for years, even generations, until disturbed. A seemingly innocuous act, such as moving the object to a different room, relocating it to another house, or gifting it to a new owner, can awaken the malevolence within.

The true danger of these infested items lies in their ability to act as a conduit for the demon's malevolence to spread. Such artefacts are not mere curiosities but are vessels of pure evil, ready to unleash their horrors upon the unwitting and the sceptical, drawing them into a nightmarish reality from which there may be no escape.

Certain locations, particularly those with a history of violence, trauma, or occult activity, can become hotspots for demonic attachments. People who spend time in these places may experience a sense of oppression, unease, or paranormal activity. The attachment can persist even after the person leaves the location, suggesting a lingering connection.

When a demon attaches itself to a home, it manifests as a harrowing, oppressive presence, a demonic haunting that slowly consumes the very soul of the place.

Attachment is the initial, insidious phase of possession. Here, the demon expresses its interest in its chosen victim, commencing a campaign of relentless torment. At this point, it has no grip on its victim but begins its ghastly work by haunting, stalking, and gradually unveiling its terrifying presence.

The infestation process begins with the demon attaching itself to a person, object, or place, gradually exerting its influence over time. This influence can manifest in various ways, such as causing the host to experience negative emotions, unexplained illnesses, or a persistent sense of dread and unease.

One of the primary signs of a demonic attachment is the sudden onset of intense negative emotions. The individual may experience unexplained bouts of anger, depression, or anxiety. These emotions are often disproportionate to the person's circumstances and can lead to significant changes in behaviour and personality. The demon feeds off these negative emotions, growing stronger as the host becomes more destabilised.

While not as extreme as possession, attachments can still result in physical symptoms. These can include unexplained fatigue, headaches, dizziness, and other ailments that seem to have no medical cause. In some cases, the host may feel a constant sense of being watched or touched by an unseen presence.

The attached individual may exhibit unusual behaviour that is out of character. This can include a sudden interest in dark or occult subjects, withdrawal from social activities, or an inexplicable attraction to certain places or objects that seem to have a negative influence. These behaviours are often subtle at first but can escalate over time.

Freeing an Object of Infestation

When it comes to objects, one of the most effective methods to address a demonic attachment is through spiritual cleansing. This can involve rituals such as smudging with sage, the use of holy water, or prayers and blessings performed by a religious or spiritual practitioner.

One important thing to remember is that you should never give the object away or simply throw it out. Doing so merely transfers the negative energy to someone else or a new location, perpetuating the cycle of malevolence.

If you are willing to destroy the object, burning it is the most effective method. Fire has long been used in purification rituals and remains one of the most powerful ways to cleanse an item of its dark energies. To burn the object, start by lighting a fire outdoors. Once blazing, carefully place the object into the flames and let it burn. Do not interfere with the fire; allow it to burn out naturally.

After the fire has died down and the ashes have cooled, pour salt into the remains. Salt is a powerful purifying substance that ensures all evil energy is expelled from the ashes. Mix the salt and ashes together, place them in a container, and bury them as deep as possible in the ground.

The optimal place for burial is at a crossroads. Crossroads are spiritually charged locations where paths intersect and energies converge. They are believed to be sites where two realms meet, making them ideal for dispersing supernatural forces. Historically, in the British Isles, criminals who could not be buried in consecrated ground were interred at crossroads.

If the object is not flammable or cannot be burned, another option is to bury it at a crossroads or throw it into a living body of water, such as a river or the ocean. Saltwater is particularly potent, and fast-moving water is ideal for carrying away the negative energy.

If you don't want to destroy or lose the item, then there are rituals you can perform to cleanse the item. The ritual I'm about to detail requires a powerful sense of intent, focus, and faith. It is designed to harness your will and the intrinsic power of the natural elements to expel the malevolent entity from the object.

For this ritual, you will need some black candles and a way of lighting them, salt, an iron nail, water, and a bowl to pour the water into. Then choose a secluded outdoor location where you can perform the ritual undisturbed. This place could be your garden or a place of natural beauty that is meaningful to you.

Place the object in the centre of a salt circle, carefully drawn on the ground. This circle serves as a barrier, confining the malevolent entity and preventing it from escaping. Surround the object with black candles and light them. These candles symbolise the darkness you are about to confront and conquer.

Stand outside the circle, grounding yourself with slow, deep breaths. Feel the earth beneath your feet, the solid connection to the physical world anchoring you against the encroaching darkness. Close your eyes and focus, summoning every ounce of your resolve and intent. Begin the invocation with a voice that echoes with authority and power:

"By the force of my will and the power of the elements, I call forth the darkness within this object. Demon, reveal yourself and face my command."

Maintain your focus, your eyes fixed on the object as you recite a cleansing incantation, one forged from the depths of your determination.

"By the salt and the flame, by the iron and the stone, I command you, spirit of darkness, to leave this object. You have no place here. I cast you out and bind you to the void."

Dip your fingers into a bowl of salt water, a universal purifier, and flick it onto the object. Each droplet is a blade of purity, cutting through the malevolent energy and weakening the demon's hold. As the water touches the object, envision it burning the demon, driving it out with each contact. Speak with unwavering conviction:

"By the purity of this water, I expel you, demon. Leave this vessel and return to the shadows from whence you came."

Pick up an iron nail, a symbol of grounding and protection, and hold it above the object. Visualise the nail drawing out the dark energy, anchoring it away from the object. As you do, chant with increasing intensity:

"By the strength of iron and the power of my spirit, I draw you out, demon. You are not welcome here. Begone and trouble this object no more."

Move around the circle, trailing salt as you go. This creates a secondary barrier, reinforcing your command. With each step, repeat your banishment:

"In the name of my will and my power, leave this vessel and return to the abyss. You have no dominion here. Depart and be bound."

As the ritual reaches its peak, the atmosphere will shift. The oppressive presence should begin to lift, and the object may seem to lose its malevolent aura. Focus on the final expulsion, visualising the demon being cast out and bound in the abyss. Speak with finality:

"By the light within, by the force of my spirit, I banish you. This object is reclaimed. You are cast out, never to return."

Once the demon has been expelled, extinguish the black candles one by one. With each extinguished flame, state firmly:

"With this light, I seal your departure. With this darkness, I reclaim this object."

In the aftermath, cleanse the object with a final wash of salt water, ensuring all traces of the demonic encounter are removed. Dispose of the salt water outside, far from your home. Scatter remaining salt around the perimeter of your home, creating a protective barrier to prevent any return of the demonic entity.

Freeing a Location of Infestation

In the case of a house with a dormant demonic presence, the mere act of moving in can provoke the demon. Renovations or significant changes to the property can also trigger a haunting. If you find yourself facing a demonic presence in your home, the following guide will aid you in banishing the demon. This ritual draws on the primal forces of intent, focus, and the power of ritual to confront and banish malevolent entities.

Before performing the ritual, prepare yourself and the space for the confrontation. Begin by ensuring the area is cleansed of all unnecessary clutter, creating a positive space and an empty battleground where the demon has nowhere to hide.

Draw a circle on the ground using salt or chalk, marking a boundary that the demon cannot cross. This circle is your sanctuary, a sacred space where your will is law. At the North, South, East, and West points of the circle, place a black candle. Light these candles one by one, their flames flickering with an unearthly glow, casting ominous shadows that dance on the walls.

In the centre of the circle, place a bowl of salt water. Surround it with objects of power, such as crystals, iron nails, or personal talismans charged with your intent. Each item should resonate with your determination to reclaim the space from the demonic presence.

Stand within the circle, grounding yourself with deep, controlled breaths. Visualise a protective barrier rising from the circle, encasing you in an impenetrable shield of pure, unwavering will. This is your fortress, a bastion of light against the encroaching darkness.

Begin the invocation with a powerful affirmation of your intent. Speak with a voice that brooks no argument, a voice that commands the attention of the unseen:

"By the strength of my will, I command the darkness to reveal itself. I summon the shadows to the light, and I stand unyielding against the night."

Feel the energy shift as the demonic presence becomes aware of your challenge. Maintain your focus and recite a cleansing incantation, one forged from the depths of your determination:

"By the salt and the flame, by the iron and the stone, I banish you, spirit of darkness, to the void from whence you came. You have no power here. Begone, and trouble this place no more."

Dip your fingers into the salt water and flick it outward, each drop a tiny blade of purity cutting through the malignant energy. As the water splashes, envision it burning the demon, driving it back with each contact. Continue your incantation, your voice rising in strength and conviction:

"By the light within, by the force of my spirit, I cast you out, demon. Depart and be bound in the abyss, never to return."

Move clockwise around the circle, trailing salt from the bowl as you go. This creates a secondary barrier, a line of defence that reinforces your command. With each step, repeat your banishment:

"In the name of my will and my power, leave this place and do not return. I reclaim this space. It is mine, and you have no dominion here."

As you complete the circle, return to the centre and extinguish the black candles one by one. With each extinguished flame, state firmly:

"With this light, I seal your departure. With this darkness, I reclaim my peace."

The room will gradually fall into deeper shadows, yet these shadows are now your allies, voids that swallow the last remnants of the demon's presence.

Stand in silence for a moment, feeling the energy settle. The oppressive weight should lift, replaced by a calm, assertive stillness. Know that the ritual is complete, the demon cast out by the force of your intent and the power of your actions.

In the aftermath, dispose of the salt water outside, far from your home, and scatter the remaining salt around the perimeter of your home, creating a barrier against any future incursions.

Deliver me, o mighty Satan, from all past error and delusion. Fill me with truth, wisdom, and understanding.

The Possessed and the Purified

Possession is one of the most chilling and complex manifestations of demonic activity, where a malevolent entity infiltrates and takes control of a human body for its own sinister purposes.

Thankfully, true possessions are exceedingly rare, but when they occur, the victims are generally the weak, emotionally unstable, and susceptible. Demons are drawn to negative, unhappy atmospheres—homes filled with resentment, arguments, or poor living conditions.

Demons possess the living to gain their victim's soul, allowing them to walk the earth and perform evil deeds. A possessed individual is slowly broken down psychologically and physically, often driven to extreme despair or suicide, enabling the demon to claim their soul.

A possession generally begins with an infestation, which involves the demon making its presence known through subtle and progressively disturbing phenomena. The victim might experience poltergeist activity—objects moving, strange noises, and unsettling sensations. Nightmares and a pervasive sense of dread often accompany these disturbances, setting the stage for further intrusion.

As the demon strengthens its foothold, it progresses to oppression. During this stage, the entity begins to attack the victim more directly. Physical ailments, such as unexplained bruises, scratches, and a general decline in health, are common. The demon also intensifies its psychological warfare, exacerbating feelings of anxiety, depression, and isolation. Relationships may deteriorate, and the victim often feels an overwhelming sense of hopelessness.

In the obsession stage, the demon exerts a significant influence over the victim's thoughts and behaviours. The individual becomes preoccupied with the demonic presence, unable to focus on anything else. Intrusive thoughts, often violent or blasphemous in nature, plague the mind, and the victim may start to exhibit erratic and self-destructive behaviours. Sleep deprivation and extreme paranoia are hallmarks of this stage, further weakening the individual's mental and emotional defences.

Without timely intervention, a demon may fully possess its victim, seizing control of both body and mind. At this advanced stage, extreme behavioural changes often occur suddenly, marked by violence, profanity, and sexual deviance. The afflicted individual exhibits violent reactions to religious symbols, scriptures, and places of worship, as though repelled by the divine.

As possession deepens, the possessed may speak in tongues or languages they have never learned, including archaic and long-forgotten dialects. Their voice can transform, becoming guttural and inhuman, resonating with an eerie, otherworldly timbre. They might display superhuman strength, far beyond normal human limits, and reveal knowledge of hidden or distant events, showcasing the demon's unholy insight.

In rarer, more severe cases, the demon's influence can contort the victim's body, distorting their appearance. Their eyes and facial expressions take on a malevolent cast, unsettling in their unnaturalness. Wounds, scars, bruises, and burns may manifest spontaneously, often in the form of sinister symbols like inverted crosses, trios of scratches, or the dreaded number six. The victim's body might twist and bend in excruciating, impossible ways, defying the bounds of human anatomy.

Victims of possession frequently report lapses in time or periods of blackout, with no memory of their actions during these intervals. Persistent, disturbing thoughts and images plague their minds, relentless and uncontrollable.

Possession is a harrowing ordeal, epitomising the pinnacle of demonic malevolence. At its worst, it drives victims to engage in self-destructive behaviour, including self-harm and suicidal ideation, as the demon seeks to utterly ruin the host it inhabits.

Ridding a person of a demon is a profoundly intense endeavour that requires absolute focus and unwavering intent. Exorcism is a deeply sacred and often terrifying ritual, steeped in religious tradition and cultural significance. It is a practice designed to expel evil spirits or demons from a person, which throughout history has been a crucial aspect of many religions, most notably within Christianity.

There are instances of willing possession, known as "perfect possession," usually resulting from a summoning ritual or a pact with a demon. In these cases, exorcising the demon is nearly impossible.

Exorcism is observed across many religions, each with its own unique methods and rituals. In Christianity, the roots of exorcism trace back to Jesus Christ's teachings, with the Catholic Church formalising the rite as a structured ceremony involving prayers, blessings, and holy objects.

Judaism also has exorcism practices where rabbis expel dybbuks, malevolent spirits, using specific prayers and sacred texts. Islamic exorcism, or Ruqyah, employs Quranic recitations and holy water to combat jinn and demons.

In Hinduism, exorcism rituals involve mantras, prayers, and sacred objects to expel evil spirits, often performed in temples dedicated to deities like Hanuman or Kali. Tibetan Buddhism features intricate ceremonies led by monks, using sacred texts and ritual instruments to restore harmony.

Shamanic traditions worldwide involve shamans using drumming, chanting, and trance states to expel harmful spirits. These diverse practices illustrate the widespread belief in exorcisms and the universal effort to confront and dispel malevolent forces across various cultures and religions.

Despite the differences in rituals and beliefs, a common thread runs through all these traditions: the importance of faith in combating evil. The Church may claim exclusivity over exorcisms, but the truth is demons do not adhere to the confines of one religion. Exorcisms are not limited to a single faith. They are effective across various belief systems and can be performed by anyone, even a layperson.

The strength of your belief system, the power of your spiritual convictions, is what drives the demons away. Whether you draw upon God, a guardian spirit, or your own positive energy, it is your inner strength and faith that will command the demons to depart.

If performed without compassion, respect, and sensitivity, it could exacerbate the situation. There are some critical things you should establish before proceeding with such a ritual. First and foremost, be sure that the individual genuinely requires an exorcism and obtain their explicit and direct consent. You must be absolutely certain that their situation is the result of demonic possession before moving forward and that they want to proceed. An unneeded or unwanted ritual can worsen their condition.

You should also ensure that the person is mentally and emotionally stable enough to endure the process. Even with explicit permission and a confirmed demonic presence, the victim must be strong enough to handle the ritual without it causing further harm. Consult the individual calmly and honestly to clarify these points. Remove all doubt and avoid pressuring or rushing them.

A significant aspect of an exorcism is evaluating the victim's claims and ensuring they are not suffering from mental health issues, epileptic fits, or psychotic episodes. If you can rule out supernatural causes, support them in seeking appropriate help.

Traditionally, if a person refused an exorcism, the exorcist might take this as the demon's influence and proceed regardless. However, exorcisms without consent often become violent, aggressive, and terrifying for the victim. This is never acceptable. An exorcism should never be violent or aggressive. Physical contact with the possessed is unnecessary. If the person needs help but refuses assistance, encourage them to speak to a professional or a trusted friend or family member who can find alternative help.

Once you have confirmed that the victim is mentally and emotionally stable, you are ready to confront the darkness with unwavering resolve and focused energy. You can reclaim the body and soul of the afflicted, banishing the demon to the abyss and restoring peace and balance.

Begin by choosing a location free from distractions at a time of day when there is unlikely to be interruptions. It should be somewhere where both you and the victim of the possession feel safe and comfortable.

The person afflicted by the demon should be seated or lying down within a protective circle drawn with salt or chalk. This circle is a sacred space, a barrier that contains the energy of the ritual and protects the surroundings. Surround the person with objects of power—crystals, iron nails, or personal talismans charged with protective intent. Each item should resonate with the force of your will and the intent to drive out the darkness.

Stand at the edge of the circle, grounding yourself with slow, deep breaths. Visualise a powerful shield of light surrounding both you and the person afflicted—a barrier that repels the demonic presence. Close your eyes and focus, summoning every ounce of your resolve. Begin the invocation with a voice that allows no defiance, a voice that commands authority and strength:

"By the force of my will and the power of my spirit, I call forth the shadows. Reveal yourself, demon, and prepare to face the light."

The demon will be aware of the challenge and may resist. Do not waver. Continue with a cleansing incantation, one forged from the depths of your determination:

"By the light within me and the force that binds the stars, I command you, spirit of darkness, to show yourself. You have no place here. By the salt and the flame, by the iron and the stone, I banish you from this vessel."

Dip your fingers into a bowl of salt water and flick it onto the person, each drop a blade of purity cutting through the malignant energy. As the water touches them, envision it burning the demon, driving it back with each contact. Speak with unwavering conviction:

"By the purity of this water, I cast you out, demon. You have no power here. Leave this body and return to the void from whence you came."

Place your hands above the person, not touching but hovering just above their body. Feel the energy emanating from them, the dark tendrils of the demon's influence. Draw upon the strength of your intent and visualise pulling these tendrils away, stripping the demon of its hold. As you do, chant with increasing intensity:

"By the strength of my spirit and the purity of my will, I draw you out, demon. You are not welcome here. Begone and trouble this soul no more."

Move your hands in a sweeping motion, as if brushing away the darkness, and continue to flick salt water onto the person. The combination of your intent, the physical actions, and the ritual words work together to weaken the demon's grip. Continue your chant:

"In the name of my will and my power, leave this vessel and return to the abyss. You have no dominion here. Depart and be bound."

As the ritual reaches its peak, the atmosphere will shift. The oppressive presence should begin to lift, and the person may show signs of relief. Focus on the final expulsion, visualising the demon being cast out and bound in the abyss. Speak with finality:

"By the light within, by the force of my spirit, I banish you. This body is reclaimed. You are cast out, never to return."

In the aftermath, recite protective prayers or affirmations, reinforcing the expulsion and fortifying their spirit against future incursions. Ensure that the space is also thoroughly cleansed. Use holy water, sage, or other purifying substances to purify the area, banishing any residual negative energies.

In nomine diaboli, ego invoco te, Lucifer. Audite vocem meam et appare. Pactum offero, animum meum pro desideriis meis.

Above: You can't become a demonologist overnight. I've been studying for decades and have a library full of book dedicated to demonology, witchcraft, and black magic.

Below: Arming yourself with the tools of trade is also important. For me it's my book containing my incantations and my trademark decorative crucifix.

Above: Here I am joined by members of the public using a Ouija board at Chatham docks on a public ghost hunting event.

Below: Stood by my lake, reflecting on how water serves as a powerful conductor of dark energy.

I invoke thee, Azazel, from the South, ancient spirit of rebellion. Imbue me with your fire and courage to break the chains of ignorance and oppression.

Legends of the Damned

There are several notable cases of demonic attachment and possession that have captured public attention and sparked significant interest and debate within the paranormal community. These cases are often well-documented and have been the subject of numerous books, films, and scholarly investigations.

The Annabelle Doll

One of the most infamous cases of demonic attachment involves the Annabelle doll, which gained widespread notoriety through the investigations of paranormal researchers Ed and Lorraine Warren. In the early 1970s, a nursing student received the doll as a gift and soon began experiencing strange occurrences. The doll appeared to move on its own, and notes with disturbing messages were found around the house. A psychic medium revealed that the doll was possessed by a demon masquerading as a young girl named Annabelle. The Warrens intervened and concluded that the doll was indeed a conduit for a malevolent entity. Annabelle was placed in a specially secured case in the Warrens' Occult Museum, where it remains to this day.

The Exorcism of Anneliese Michel

One of the most infamous possession cases is that of Anneliese Michel, a German woman who underwent 67 exorcisms in 1975-1976. Anneliese began experiencing severe depression and hallucinations in her teenage years, which modern medicine attributed to epilepsy and mental illness. However, she and her deeply religious family believed she was possessed by multiple demons, including Lucifer, Judas Iscariot, Nero, Cain, and Hitler. The exorcisms, conducted by two priests, were intense and gruelling but ultimately unsuccessful in saving Anneliese. She died of malnutrition and dehydration in 1976. The case led to legal proceedings against her parents and the priests, and it has inspired films such as 'The Exorcism of Emily Rose'.

The Doris Bither Case

Also known as the Entity Case, this is a well-documented and terrifying account of demonic attachment involving a woman named Doris Bither in the 1970s. Bither claimed that she and her children were being attacked by unseen forces in their home in Culver City, California. The most disturbing aspect of the case was the physical assaults, which included sexual attacks by invisible entities. A team of paranormal researchers, including Dr. Barry Taff and Kerry Gaynor, investigated the house and witnessed inexplicable phenomena, including balls of light and physical manifestations. Despite their efforts, the haunting continued, and Bither eventually moved away, but the case remains one of the most harrowing examples of demonic attachment.

The Exorcism of Roland Doe

The case of Roland Doe (a pseudonym for the boy involved, whose real name was Robbie Mannheim), also known as the St. Louis exorcism case, is one of the most famous instances of possession. This case involved a 14-year-old boy in the late 1940s who began experiencing strange phenomena after his aunt introduced him to a Ouija board. The boy's family reported furniture moving on its own, strange noises, and objects levitating. After consulting their Lutheran pastor, the family turned to the Catholic Church. The exorcisms were performed by Father William Bowdern and Father Walter Halloran. During the rituals, Roland exhibited violent reactions, spoke in a guttural voice, and displayed knowledge of events and languages he could not have known. The final exorcism concluded with Roland declaring he was free from the demonic presence. This case served as the basis for William Peter Blatty's novel 'The Exorcist'.

The Amityville Horror

The Amityville Horror is one of the most famous cases of demonic attachment linked to a specific location. In 1974, Ronald DeFeo Jr. murdered six members of his family in their home at 112 Ocean Avenue in Amityville, New York. The following year, the Lutz family moved into the house but fled after only 28 days, claiming they experienced intense paranormal activity. The Lutzes reported phenomena such as swarms of flies, cold spots, foul odours, and green slime oozing from the walls. George Lutz claimed to have seen demonic faces and felt an oppressive presence throughout the house. The case was investigated by various paranormal experts, including Ed and Lorraine Warren, who concluded that the house was plagued by demonic entities. The Amityville Horror has since become a cultural phenomenon, inspiring numerous books and films.

The Bell Witch

The Bell Witch haunting is an early American case of attachment that took place in Adams, Tennessee, in the early 19th century. The Bell family began experiencing strange noises, physical attacks, and sightings of a spectral figure. The entity seemed particularly hostile towards John Bell and his daughter Betsy. The Bell

Witch, as it became known, was said to be a malevolent spirit capable of speech, physical assault, and manipulating objects. The haunting persisted for several years and ended mysteriously with the death of John Bell, which some attributed to the witch.

Many believe the Bell Witch was more than a mere ghost or restless spirit. The entity's sheer malevolence, its ability to manipulate the physical environment, and its profound intelligence suggest the presence of a demonic force. Demons are known for their cunning, their desire to inflict suffering, and their ability to manifest in numerous forms. The Bell Witch displayed all these characteristics, leading many to conclude that a demon was indeed at work.

The Smurl Haunting

The Smurl family haunting in West Pittston, Pennsylvania, is another chilling case. Jack and Janet Smurl, along with their children, experienced a decade-long haunting starting in 1974, which they attributed to demonic possession. The family reported foul smells, strange noises, physical attacks, and the appearance of shadowy figures. The case gained notoriety when paranormal investigators Ed and Lorraine Warren were called in. The Warrens claimed the Smurl home was occupied by a powerful demon. Despite multiple exorcisms, the disturbances continued until the family eventually moved.

The Perron Family Haunting

The Perron family haunting, which inspired the film 'The Conjuring', involved a demonic attachment in their farmhouse in Harrisville, Rhode Island. In the 1970s, the Perron family began experiencing a range of paranormal phenomena, including strange noises, foul odours, and physical attacks. The mother, Carolyn Perron, was particularly targeted, suffering from severe physical and psychological torment. Ed and Lorraine Warren investigated the case and identified the primary malevolent entity as Bathsheba Sherman, a witch who had lived in the area during the 19th century. The Warrens performed multiple cleansing rituals, but the haunting left a lasting impact on the family, who eventually moved out.

The Ammons Haunting

A more recent case is the Ammons haunting, which took place in Gary, Indiana, in 2011. Latoya Ammons and her three children reported being tormented by demons in their home. The family experienced strange occurrences such as swarms of flies, shadowy figures, and the levitation of one of the children. The case gained significant attention when medical professionals, including a child services caseworker and a hospital staff, claimed to have witnessed the paranormal activity. The family sought help from their church, and multiple exorcisms were performed by Father Michael Maginot. The case was widely covered in the media and became the subject of a documentary.

The Black Monk of Pontefract

The Black Monk of Pontefract is widely recognised as one of the most violent and well-documented cases of demonic attachment in the United Kingdom. In the late 1960s, the Pritchard family moved into a house in Pontefract, West Yorkshire, and soon began experiencing disturbing paranormal activity. The entity, dubbed the "Black Monk," was responsible for physical attacks, levitating objects, and other malevolent phenomena. The haunting was characterised by its intensity and the physical harm inflicted on family members, particularly the teenage daughter, Diane. The Black Monk of Pontefract is believed to be the spirit of a 16th-century monk who was executed for heinous crimes. Despite various attempts to cleanse the house, the activity reportedly continues, making it a notorious site for paranormal investigators.

My first encounter with the Black Monk of Pontefract was during the two-part 'Most Haunted' special that aired in early October 2015. The moment I set foot inside 30 East Drive, the malevolent energy was palpable, as though the very walls whispered of ancient darkness. The investigation was fraught with occurrences that defied rational explanation and left even the seasoned 'Most Haunted' team unnerved.

One incident, in particular, stands out in my memory. While filming in the living room, we noticed a large kitchen knife had inexplicably moved, finding itself wedged between the sofa cushions. A review of the footage revealed no sign of the knife mere moments before, underscoring the entity's ability to manipulate the physical environment with a sinister precision.

The tension reached its peak during the 'Most Haunted Live: A Nightmare on East Drive' Halloween special later that month, the first live investigation Yvette had led the team on since 2010. In an effort to safeguard the team, Karl placed the knife inside a box, locking it in front of a camera to ensure it couldn't surprise us again. Yet, as if mocking our precautions, the knife was later discovered on the bed in the master bedroom. When Karl went to retrieve it, the knife had vanished again, only to reappear after a loud crash in the living room, lying ominously against the skirting board. These eerie occurrences compelled us to remove not just the knife but the entire cutlery drawer from the house.

Later in the night, I joined the investigation. Until that point, I had been outside performing incantations, a ritual I believed had agitated the dark forces within the house and sparked the knife's dangerous movements. I was brought into the house in time for midnight, the climax of the show, to perform a final, powerful ritual.

At the stroke of midnight, I stood at the foot of the stairs and began reciting powerful incantations while ancient Hebrew chants of the Lord's Prayer resonated throughout the house via loudspeakers. The atmosphere grew thick with a foreboding presence as I called upon the dark forces:

"In nomine Dei nostri Satanas Luciferi excelsi. In the name of Satan, ruler of the Earth, true God almighty. I invite the forces of darkness to bestow their infernal power upon me. Open the gates of hell to come forth and greet me as your brother and friend. Deliver me, o mighty Satan, from all past error and delusion. Fill me with truth, wisdom, and understanding. I invoke thee, Lucifer, from the East. I invoke thee, Beelzebub, from the North. I invoke thee, Astaroth, from the West. I invoke thee, Azazel, from the South. Come forward, forces of darkness, and greet me."

As the incantations reverberated through the house, the team was gathered around a table upstairs. The atmosphere was electric with anticipation and dread.

Suddenly, Karl leapt up, shouting in terror, and bolted down the stairs. Pushing me aside, he exclaimed, "This house is fucking nuts!" as he hurriedly made his way out of the house. After calming down, he recounted feeling as though he had been punched in the side, an invisible force driving fear and pain into him.

I favour the just and curse the rotten. By all the gods of the pit, I command that these things of which I speak shall come to pass.

Opening the Gates of Hell

Invoking a demon, the act of calling upon demons to come forward, is not for the faint of heart. It is by far the blackest of all the black arts. Traditionally, summoning demons was an act fraught with peril, often undertaken to form sinister pacts for personal gain, wealth, to answer questions, or to curse an enemy with pain and suffering.

You don't need specific skills, psychic powers, or prior experience to summon a demon, but you must approach the act responsibly. Demons have a tendency to attach themselves to or follow those who summon them, so it's crucial to ensure they return to their realm after the session. We'll explore this further later. A summoning can be elaborate and ritualistic or as simple as sitting alone in a darkened room and commanding the demon with your voice.

As a demonologist, I have spent countless hours studying and practicing the ancient art of summoning demons. This practice, rooted in deep tradition and ritual, is not for the faint-hearted. It requires precision, respect, and a firm understanding of the forces you are dealing with. Although I have tried and tested incantations that I draw upon, the power lies not in the words themselves but in the belief and intent behind them.

I've become known for my now-famous incantations. On television, they are often muted by the channel, so you don't get the whole thing because it can be quite dangerous. These chants come from a large book of shadows I often use, and I will share these chants with you now.

I use these incantations because they have a proven track record of causing paranormal activity to occur, something which I thrive on experiencing, and also make great viewing for fans of the TV show. However, my chanting and the activity it leads to often unsettles my fellow team members. Darren Hutchinson, our sound man, particularly dislikes being alone with me during these sessions. In one episode at Haden Hill House, Darren was visibly terrified when I started chanting. Despite Darren's protests, I continued, unfazed by the unexplained sounds that followed. In another episode at Standon Hall, my incantation prompted Darren to flee from the building.

As I prepare to recite an incantation, confidence and clarity are key. Each word must be spoken with conviction, for supernatural forces respond to the strength of your intent and the precision of the command. A wavering voice or uncertain heart can weaken the ritual, but a clear and powerful invocation can pierce the veil and summon dark forces.

For me, these incantations are a deeply personal and spiritual experience. It is a moment of connection with the infernal, a declaration of my commitment to the path I have chosen. Each time I utter these words, I feel the energy shift, the air grow thick with power, and the presence of the dark forces drawing near.

I normally open my incantations with one of the following lines:

"In nomine Dei nostri Satanas Luciferi excelsi."

Translation: Satan the morning star of the Most High in the name of our God.

"In nomine patris et filii et spiritus sancti."

Translation: In the name of the Father and of the Son, and the Holy Spirit.

"Procedamus in pace, in nomine Christi, Amen."

Translation: Let us go forth in peace, in the name of Christ, Amen.

These lines are a variation of a verse that originates from the annals of the Church of Satan, founded by Anton LaVey in 1966. LaVey, a master of the dark arts and a pivotal figure in modern Satanism, crafted these words to encapsulate the essence of his philosophy. The Church of Satan sought to strip away the hypocritical veneer of conventional religions, embracing instead the primal, carnal nature of humanity. This incantation, therefore, is a bold declaration of allegiance to Satan, the ultimate symbol of rebellion and enlightenment.

I'll break down the full 'Invocation to Satan' and its meaning, but first, here is the full version from LaVey's text, which is as follows:

In nomine Dei nostri Satanas Luciferi excelsi.

In the name of Satan, the Ruler of the earth, the King of the world, I command the forces of Darkness to bestow their Infernal power upon me.

Open wide the gates of Hell and come forth from the abyss to greet me as your brother (sister) and friend.

Grant me the indulgences of which I speak.

I have taken thy name as a part of myself. I live as the beasts of the field, rejoicing in the fleshly life. I favor the just and curse the rotten.

By all the Gods of the Pit, I command that these things of which I speak shall come to pass.

Come forth and answer to your names by manifesting my desires.

The incantation, "In nomine Dei nostri Satanas Luciferi excelsi," is not merely a string of words but a resonant call to the ancient forces that dwell beyond the veil of our mundane existence. This invocation, rooted deeply in the rich soil of occult tradition, serves as a bridge between our world and the infernal realms, summoning the raw, unfiltered power of Satan and his dark legions.

"In the name of Satan, the Ruler of the earth, the King of the world, I command the forces of Darkness to bestow their Infernal power upon me." These words are an unequivocal summons, calling forth the forces of Hell to aid and empower the practitioner. They recognise Satan not only as the ruler of the infernal realms but also as the true sovereign of our earthly existence, a stark contrast to the benign deities of other faiths. In this invocation, we acknowledge his dominion and seek to draw upon his boundless power.

"Open wide the gates of Hell and come forth from the abyss to greet me as your brother (sister) and friend." This line is a call for unity and kinship with the infernal forces. It is an invitation for these entities to recognise the practitioner as one of their own, a bold step into the dark brotherhood that transcends the mortal coil. The gates of Hell, symbolic of the boundary between our world and the abyss, are asked to open, allowing these powerful entities to manifest and offer their guidance and support.

"Grant me the indulgences of which I speak. I have taken thy name as a part of myself. I live as the beasts of the field, rejoicing in the fleshly life." Here, we ask for the fulfilment of our desires, recognising that in taking Satan's name, we embrace a life unshackled by the constraints of conventional morality. To live as the beasts of the field is to embrace our true nature, to revel in the pleasures of the flesh without shame or restraint. It is a celebration of the primal, unadulterated life that Satanism advocates.

"I favor the just and curse the rotten. By all the Gods of the Pit, I command that these things of which I speak shall come to pass." This passage is a declaration of our own moral compass, one that favours justice as we perceive it and curses the corrupt and the wicked. By invoking all the gods of the pit, we draw upon a vast reservoir of dark power, commanding that our desires and intentions be made manifest in the world.

"Come forth and answer to your names by manifesting my desires." The final command is a direct call to the infernal entities to respond and bring our will into reality. It is a demand for action, for the tangible manifestation of our deepest desires, leveraging the ancient and formidable power of the dark forces.

You may have also heard me use the following incantation, mostly notably during that infamous live broadcast in Pontefract:

"Deliver me, o mighty Satan, from all past error and delusion, fill me with truth, wisdom, and understanding. I invoke thee, Lucifer from the East. I invoke thee, Beelzebub from the North. I invoke thee, Astaroth from the West. I invoke thee, Azazel from the South. Come forward forces of darkness and greet me."

This particular passage is derived from modern ceremonial magic and theistic Satanism. It is often found within texts and rituals associated with the Church of Satan and other similar organisations dedicated to the veneration of Satan and the demonic hierarchy.

The invocation itself is a powerful plea to the four cardinal directions, calling upon Lucifer from the East, Beelzebub from the North, Astaroth from the West, and Azazel from the South. Each of these entities holds significant power and influence within the demonic realm, and summoning them together in such a manner is a profound and dangerous act.

Lucifer, often regarded as the bringer of light and enlightenment, represents the quest for truth and wisdom. Beelzebub, the Lord of the Flies, embodies corruption and decay, often associated with the sins of gluttony and pride. Astaroth, a grand duke of Hell, is known for her wisdom and guidance in matters of science and philosophy. Azazel, a fallen angel, is synonymous with rebellion and is often linked with the introduction of forbidden knowledge to humanity.

This invocation is not one to be taken lightly. It demands respect and an unwavering belief in the forces being called upon. Those who dare to utter these words must be prepared for the consequences, as the summoned entities may not be benign or forgiving. The forces of darkness are not to be trifled with, and such an invocation is a bold declaration of one's commitment to the path of the left-hand.

Here is a full version of 'The Invocation of the Four Princes of Hell' as found in shadowy occult texts. It serves as a gateway to immense power and understanding, but it also comes with great risk:

Deliver me, o mighty Satan, from all past error and delusion. Fill me with truth, wisdom, and understanding.

I invoke thee, Lucifer, from the East, bringer of light and knowledge. Illuminate my path with your wisdom and grant me insight beyond mortal comprehension.

I invoke thee, Beelzebub, from the North, mighty prince of the infernal empire. Grant me strength and power to overcome all obstacles and adversaries that stand in my way.

I invoke thee, Astaroth, from the West, great duke of Hell and keeper of secrets. Bestow upon me your profound knowledge and guide me in the ways of the arcane.

I invoke thee, Azazel, from the South, ancient spirit of rebellion. Imbue me with your fire and courage to break the chains of ignorance and oppression.

Come forward, forces of darkness, and greet me. Embrace me as your servant and ally in the eternal quest for truth and power. Let your presence be known and felt within this sacred space.

By the power of the infernal, by the flame that burns eternally, I command and conjure thee to appear before me.

So mote it be.

The Standard Satanic Ritual and the Advanced Satanic Ritual, which follow, serve as the cornerstones for practitioners, whether they are novices or seasoned adepts. These rituals are designed to invoke the presence of Satan. For whichever of the rituals you choose to perform, you should begin by preparing yourself, both physically and mentally. You can do this by meditating or taking a bath or shower to purify your body and mind in respect for the sacred rite you are about to perform.

Setting the right mood is essential to increasing your chances of summoning a demon. Hold your ritual in low light or by candlelight, avoiding complete darkness. Burning incense can help, but steer clear of sage as it repels evil energies. Ensure you're comfortable, as making contact with a demon requires time and patience. Eliminate distractions by silencing your phone and shutting out pets and other interruptions.

The optimal time to summon demons is between 3 and 4 am, known as the witching hour, or "high noon" of the demonic day. While dusk till dawn, around 9 pm to 5 am, is paranormally active, 3 am is considered the peak time for demonic activity.

Setting clear intentions and boundaries is paramount. You should know precisely what you wish to achieve and be ready to enforce these boundaries during the interaction. Ambiguity or indecision can be exploited by the demon, so clarity and determination are crucial.

As your session with the demon draws to a close, it is crucial to ensure that the entity does not linger. Even if you believe your summoning was unsuccessful, always err on the side of caution. There is always the possibility that something was indeed summoned, but it chose to remain silent or hidden.

It is also essential to verbally command the demon to depart. As you conclude the session, address the demon directly: "Thank you for making yourself known to me. You must now return to the realm you came from. You cannot stay here." Employ the cleansing and protective techniques discussed earlier to drive the demon away. Smudging with sage, drawing protective salt circles, or invoking your protective talismans are all effective methods.

The Standard Satanic Ritual

Before you begin, fill a silver chalice with wine or another suitable drink. You will also need a pen and paper, a candle, and a ritual bell. The bell should be small and made of a resonant metal, suitable for creating a clear, lingering sound. After lighting the candle, face the East with your left index finger held aloft and call upon Satan:

"Satan, ruler of the East, I call upon you."

Visualise a stream of electric blue light entering your left index finger, filling your being and connecting you to the infernal power. Turn to the North, feeling the energy intensify, and proclaim:

"Beelzebub, ruler of the North, I call upon you."

Next, turn to the West, allowing the infernal power to build, and call upon Astaroth with the words:

"Astaroth, ruler of the West, I call upon you."

Finally, complete the circle by turning to the South and invoking Azazel by saying:

"Azazel, ruler of the South, I call upon you."

Feel the combined might of the Four Crowned Princes of Hell coursing through you. Hold your left index finger aloft once more and recite this version of the 'Invocation to Satan':

"In nomine Dei nostri Satanas Luciferi excelsi. In the name of Satan, the Ruler of the earth, the King of the world, I command the forces of Darkness to bestow their Infernal power upon me. Open wide the gates of Hell and come forth from the abyss to greet me as your brother (sister) and friend.

Deliver me, o mighty Satan, from all past error and delusion. Fill me with truth, wisdom, and understanding. Keep me strong in my faith and service, that I may abide always in Thee, with Praise, Honour, and Glory be given Thee forever and ever."

Drink deeply from the chalice, signifying your acceptance of Satan's power into your being. As the infernal energy permeates your soul, write your prayers, thanksgivings, and requests on clean paper. Burn the paper in the flame of your candle, watching the smoke rise and carry your words to the infernal realms. Enter a state of deep meditation, focusing on your desires and visualising them manifesting in the physical world. Feel the energy of Satan and his demons flowing through you, amplifying your intent.

Conclude the ritual by giving thanks to Satan and any demons you have called upon. Ring the bell once, turn clockwise, and proclaim:

"Hail Satan!"

Dispose of the burned remains in a manner befitting the gravity of the ritual, such as flushing them down the toilet or burying them.

The Advanced Satanic Ritual

The Advanced Satanic Ritual delves deeper into the esoteric, utilising the full spectrum of elemental and spiritual forces to achieve profound transformations and manifestations.

Begin by preparing your ritual space, ensuring you have all the necessary tools at hand, including a candle, a silver chalice filled with wine or another suitable drink, a small resonant bell, incense, a pen, and some paper. Before you start, light the incense and your candle.

The ritual begins with the ringing of the bell, symbolising reverberation and the activation of the spiritual realm. The sound of the bell is not merely to mark the commencement; it is a call to the infernal forces, a vibration that sets the tone for the ritual. Hold the bell up and ring it once, allowing its clear, resonant sound to fill the environment, signalling the beginning of the rite and awakening the energies.

Next, stand before your altar and raise your left index finger in the air. This is the time to call upon the elements, which are represented by the Four Crowned Princes of Hell. Face the East and invoke Air:

"Spirits of Air, I call upon you. Enter my being and fill me with your clarity and knowledge. Align my soul with the winds of change and breath of life."

Turn to the South and invoke Fire:

"Spirits of Fire, I call upon you. Enter my being and ignite my spirit with your passion and power. Align my soul with the flames of transformation and desire."

Next, turn to the West and invoke Water:

"Spirits of Water, I call upon you. Enter my being and cleanse my soul with your purity and intuition. Align my soul with the currents of emotion and flow of the unseen."

Turn to the North and invoke Earth:

"Spirits of Earth, I call upon you. Enter my being and ground my spirit with your strength and stability. Align my soul with the solidity of the material and the foundation of all things."

Finally, centre yourself and invoke Ether:

"Spirits of Ether, I call upon you. Enter my being and unify my spirit with your essence of the cosmos. Align my soul with the infinite and the void from which all power flows."

Feel each element's force merging with your being, empowering your soul and aligning you with the natural forces. Hold your index finger up again and recite the 'Invocation to Satan':

"In nomine Dei nostri Satanas Luciferi excelsi. In the name of Satan, the Ruler of the earth, the King of the world, I command the forces of Darkness to bestow their Infernal power upon me. Open wide the gates of Hell and come forth from the abyss to greet me as your brother/sister and friend. Grant me the indulgences of which I speak. I have taken thy name as a part of myself. I live as the beasts of the field, rejoicing in the fleshly life. I favour the just and curse the rotten. By all the Gods of the Pit, I command that these things of which I speak shall come to pass. Come forth and answer to your names by manifesting my desires."

Reach for your silver chalice and drink deeply, signifying your acceptance of Satan's power into your being. As the infernal energy permeates your soul, sit quietly for a few minutes to ensure you receive a powerful energy buzz, enhancing the effectiveness of the working. This step ensures that your soul is at full power, ready for the manifestation of your desires.

Write your prayers, thanksgivings, and requests on clean paper. Focus and concentrate on your desires, directing the energies of your soul into the working. Burn the paper in the flame of your candle, watching the smoke rise and carry your words to the infernal realms. Fire symbolises the spark of life and transformation, essential for directing your energies into the working.

Visualise your goal with intense clarity. Hold the image of your desire firmly in your mind, feeling the power you have invoked flowing into it and bringing it into existence. Close the ritual by affirming your faith in

Satan and expressing gratitude for the power bestowed upon you. Speak these words with conviction:

"Mighty Satan, I thank you for the power and guidance you have granted me. May your infernal will be done through me. I affirm my faith in you and pledge my continued devotion. Hail Satan!"

Ring the ritual bell once more, signalling the end of the ceremony. Feel the bond between you and the infernal forces solidifying, ensuring their continued favour and guidance.

I call upon the shadows, the hidden ones who dwell beyond the veil. Hear our call, Lilith, queen of the night. Asmodeus, lord of desire, we invoke thee. Lend your power to our rite, as we merge and create.

A Pact with the Devil

As a demonologist, I have studied many forms of dark magic, but few are as infamous or as feared as making a pact with the Devil, sometimes referred to as "perfect possession." This ancient practice involves striking a solemn and binding deal with the Devil or one of his lesser demons, offering one's soul in exchange for diabolical favours.

For some, it is the insatiable hunger for power, the desire to rise above all others, to command legions and bend the world to their will. The Devil offers dominion, a taste of divine authority, allowing the pact-maker to wield influence and control far beyond their mortal capacity. Others are driven by the quest for forbidden knowledge, secrets that lie hidden in the abyssal depths of the occult. Scholars, magicians, and seekers of arcane wisdom may find themselves at the Devil's doorstep, yearning for the enlightenment that only the infernal can bestow. The promise of understanding the mysteries of the universe, mastering the dark arts, and unlocking the secrets of life and death lures them into the Devil's grasp.

Throughout history, many individuals, driven by desperation, ambition, or curiosity, have claimed to have made pacts with the Devil. The legendary blues musician Robert Johnson, for instance, is said to have met the Devil at a crossroads in rural Mississippi, signing over his soul to acquire his extraordinary guitar skills. This story, steeped in the mystique of the Delta Blues, suggests that Johnson exchanged his soul for musical prowess, transforming him into one of the greatest blues musicians of all time. His life, shrouded in mystery, and his untimely death at the age of 27 only added to the legend, intertwining his name forever with the dark lore of the crossroads.

Before you ask if the Devil was behind my 1970s pop career, I'll leave that up to you to decide. And if you don't know what I'm talking about, there's a video knocking around on the internet of me on a music show of the time hosted by David 'Kid' Jensen. Search for "Johnnie Ricco" and you'll see what I mean.

The practice of making a diabolical pact, while promising great rewards, comes with immense risks. It is not a decision to be taken lightly. The details must be meticulously planned, and the ritual performed with the utmost seriousness and respect. The consequences of failing to uphold your end of the bargain can be dire, as demons do not take kindly to broken promises.

The first and perhaps most crucial step on this journey is to define your purpose with unwavering precision. Contemplate deeply why you seek this dark alliance. Is it fame that you crave, the glittering allure of fortune, the intoxicating rush of power, or the sweet sting of revenge? Perhaps you yearn for eternal youth, immortality, or the elusive grasp of true love. Your desire must be singular, something beyond the reach of ordinary means. Only when your heart and mind are aligned with this longing can you identify the demon most suited to your cause.

Choosing your demon is a matter of great significance. While Satan himself is most renowned in the annals of dark pacts, there are myriad lesser demons, each with their own unique proclivities and domains. The demon Agares, for instance, is the keeper of knowledge, while Andras thrives on the fires of revenge. Asmodeus reigns over carnal desires and lust, Belial is the architect of career advancement and power, and Paimon possesses the art of control over others. Select your demonic ally with care, for each one holds dominion over different facets of human desire.

Once your demon is chosen, it is imperative to articulate the terms of your pact with crystal clarity, for the Devil is a master of semantics and will twist vague requests to his advantage. Be specific in your demands and equally precise in what you are prepared to offer in return. Often, the demon will seek something from you—perhaps the recruitment of more souls or assistance in furthering its own dark agenda.

Commit your terms to writing, for the act of writing solidifies your intentions and mitigates misunderstandings. A written pact, often inscribed in blood or red ink to underscore your earnestness, should detail your desires and offerings. This document must be signed and stored in a place of safety.

The making of your deal is best undertaken under the cloak of night when the veil between worlds is thinnest. Choose a place where you feel safe and comfortable or a location steeped in history or close to nature. Ancient forests, abandoned ruins, and desolate crossroads are particularly potent sites. Ensure that you are alone, for witnesses can disrupt the delicate balance required for such an invocation.

Before the ritual, you'll need to create your altar by arranging black candles in a pentagram, the ancient symbol of power and protection inverted to signify your intent. At the centre, place a mirror that will serve as the portal through which the Devil may manifest.

Begin by calling upon the Devil or your chosen demon by name. Treat the demon with the utmost respect, for to antagonise such an entity could invite ruin. Chant the following invocation, speaking with conviction, as the Devil respects strength and resolve:

"In nomine diaboli, ego invoco te, Lucifer. Audite vocem meam et appare. Pactum offero, animum meum pro desideriis meis."

This Latin phrase, commonly used in rituals to summon demonic entities, translates as: "In the name of the Devil, I call upon you, Lucifer. Hear my voice and appear. I offer a pact, my soul for my desires."

Repeat the chant until you feel the presence of the infernal drawing near. When the mirror darkens and a form begins to coalesce, you will know that your invocation has succeeded. Seal the pact with a blood offering. Prick your finger and let your blood drip onto the mirror, symbolising your unbreakable bond. As the blood meets the surface, you will feel a shift, a binding force that transcends the physical realm.

Alternatively, the demon might show signs of its acceptance through the moving of objects. Taps might echo in the stillness, or unearthly sounds could herald the sealing of your deal. Once the pact is sealed, extinguish the candles and express gratitude for the demon's efforts.

In the days and weeks following the ritual, you may notice an uncanny alignment of events in your favour. This is not mere coincidence but the direct influence of the pact. Wealth may flow more freely into your coffers, opportunities previously out of reach may present themselves, or individuals of influence may be drawn inexplicably to your orbit. These are the fruits of your dark bargain, the manifestations of the power you sought.

Visions and dreams serve as another harbinger of your success. In the dead of night, as you drift between the realms of wakefulness and slumber, you may encounter the Devil or his emissaries. These visions are vivid, more real than any dream, and they often carry messages or instructions. Pay heed to these nocturnal visitations, for they are a direct line of communication with your infernal benefactor.

Physical marks may also appear upon your body, unbidden and unexplained. These can take the form of scars, burns, or symbols that etch themselves into your flesh. They are the Devil's brand, a sign to the world that you are his. These marks often appear in places easily concealed but occasionally manifest where they can be glimpsed by the discerning eye.

A change in perception is another telltale sign. Your senses may sharpen, allowing you to perceive the world in a way others cannot. Colours may seem more vibrant, sounds more acute, and your intuition more pronounced. This heightened awareness is a gift from the dark forces now intertwined with your soul, a tool to aid you in your endeavours.

Behavioural changes may also be observed. You might find yourself more confident, assertive, and unafraid to take risks you once shied away from. This newfound boldness is the influence of the Devil's power, emboldening you to seize the opportunities provided by your pact.

However, these signs are not without their shadows. The price of your bargain will begin to manifest as well. Relationships may strain and fracture as loved ones sense the change in you and recoil from the darkness that now clings to your aura. Nightmares, far more terrifying than the visions, may plague your sleep, reminding you of the debt you owe.

The Devil is a master of deceit, and the fulfilment of the pact's promises often comes with unforeseen and devastating consequences. The soul that enters into such an agreement is forever marked, bound to an eternity of torment and servitude in the infernal realms.

Breaking a pact with the Devil is no small feat. While exceedingly rare and fraught with peril, there are whispered methods by which you can attempt to sever these unholy bonds. However, get it wrong, and the consequences are dire.

One of the most ancient and perilous methods to break a pact involves a direct confrontation with the infernal forces themselves. This method is fraught with danger, as it requires summoning the very entity with whom the pact was made. Armed with powerful protective charms, the pact-maker must enter into a negotiation, seeking to outwit or bargain with the Devil to release their soul.

This approach demands extraordinary cunning, courage, and a deep understanding of the demonic psyche. The Devil, ever the deceiver, will not easily relinquish a soul, and the negotiation can easily turn treacherous. Only those with the sharpest minds and steeliest wills should attempt this path.

Occasionally, a loophole may exist within the terms of the pact itself. The Devil, while cunning, is bound by the exact wording of the contract. An astute and meticulous examination of the pact might reveal an overlooked clause or condition that could be exploited to nullify the agreement. This method requires not only a keen legalistic mind but also the guidance of an expert in demonology or occult law. Finding such a loophole is exceedingly rare, but if discovered, it can provide a means of escape.

There are also certain arcane rituals and spells, buried deep within forbidden grimoires, that claim to offer a means of breaking infernal pacts. These rituals are complex and dangerous, often involving the summoning of other powerful entities to intercede on the pact-maker's behalf. The risks associated with these rituals are immense, as the summoning of such forces can easily spiral out of control, leading to catastrophic consequences. Success in this endeavour requires not only mastery of the dark arts but also a willingness to confront the unknown and potentially pay an even greater price.

By the power of the infernal, by the flame that burns eternally, I command and conjure thee to appear before me.

Sinister Sanctuaries

In the shadowed corners of our world, where history and the supernatural entwine, lie places marked by darkness and whispered secrets. These are not merely locations of ghostly apparitions but sites where demonic forces have left an indelible stain. These are some of Britain's most sinister locations, where the line between our reality and the demonic blurs and the echoes of ancient rituals still reverberate. Each site holds its own unique horrors, serving as a stark reminder of the unseen forces that linger in the shadows, waiting to make their presence known.

The Hellfire Caves, Buckinghamshire

Nestled in the heart of Buckinghamshire, the Hellfire Caves have always held a special, almost magnetic allure for me. When I was a mere 16 years old, I first ventured into these subterranean depths and felt an inexplicable connection, as though the very stones whispered secrets meant only for me.

The caves, carved into the chalk and flint hills, were commissioned by Sir Francis Dashwood in the mid-1700s. They became the notorious meeting place for the Hellfire Club, a group shrouded in scandal and whispers of debauchery. Tales of hedonistic rituals, where prostitutes dressed as nuns participated in orgies, are but a glimpse into the dark revelries that took place.

The club was rumoured to engage in Black Masses and Satanic rituals within these subterranean chambers, and these acts have left a dark mark there. Visitors often report an overwhelming sense of dread and unease, as if the shadows themselves are watching, whispering secrets of past sins and forbidden practices.

Years later, while delving into my family tree, I discovered that an ancestor of mine is buried at St. Lawrence's Church, which is perched above the caves. This revelation only deepened my connection to the caves, affirming the inexplicable bond I felt with this place of shadow and sin.

The Ancient Ram Inn, Gloucestershire

The Ancient Ram Inn in Wotton-under-Edge stands as a monument to centuries of dark history and paranormal activity. Constructed in 1145 on a pagan burial ground, the inn has been the site of numerous sinister occurrences. Among the most disturbing are encounters with an incubus and a succubus.

An incubus is a male demon believed to lie upon sleeping women to engage in sexual activity with them. These entities are said to drain the life force from their victims, leaving them weakened and tormented. The succubus, on the other hand, is a female counterpart that seduces men, often appearing in dreams to engage in sexual acts. These encounters are not merely physical but profoundly spiritual, often leaving the victim with a sense of dread and lingering fear.

Many who have dared to stay at the Ancient Ram Inn have reported being pinned down by an invisible force, feeling an oppressive weight on their chests, and waking up with scratches and bruises. These experiences are consistent with the presence of an incubus or succubus, entities that feed on the fear and energy of the living.

Drakelow Tunnels, Worcestershire

Beneath the unassuming countryside of Worcestershire lies a labyrinth of dark and eerie tunnels known as the Drakelow Tunnels. These tunnels were originally constructed during World War II as a shadow factory and later used as a nuclear bunker. However, their history stretches back much further, to a time when an ancient hill fort and its graveyard occupied the site. During the tunnelling process, hundreds of bodies were disturbed, awakening a guardian demon bound to the burial ground.

This demon is said to take the form of a half-man, half-dog creature. Visitors have felt an unseen entity brush past their legs in the darkness, leaving an icy chill in its wake. The oppressive atmosphere within the tunnels is palpable, a heavy silence broken only by the occasional, inexplicable sound of growling. This guardian demon is believed to harbour a deep resentment towards those who trespass, protecting the sanctity of the disturbed graves with a ferocity that chills the soul.

Pengersick Castle, Cornwall

Pengersick Castle, perched on the rugged Cornish coast, is a site steeped in blood and mystery. This fortress is renowned not only for its medieval architecture but also for the plethora of supernatural occurrences reported within its walls. Among the many spirits that haunt Pengersick Castle are two murdered monks, sailors searching for lost treasure, and the cries of souls buried in unhallowed graves. Most chilling, however, is the presence of a demon that has terrorised visitors and residents alike.

The demon of Pengersick Castle is a malevolent entity, said to be bound to the site by ancient, dark rituals. It manifests as a shadowy figure, often accompanied by a sudden drop in temperature and an overwhelming sense of dread. Witnesses have described the feeling of being watched by unseen eyes, and some have even reported being physically attacked by this unseen force. The demon's presence is often heralded by the pitiful cries of the damned, echoing through the cold stone corridors of the castle. These spectral wails serve as a grim reminder of the countless souls who met their end in the castle's dark history.

St. Botolph's Church, Lincolnshire

Also known as "The Demon Church," St. Botolph's in Boston, Lincolnshire, is steeped in dark history. Linked to Satanic groups in the 1970s and 80s, the now-abandoned church has become a magnet for paranormal investigators. The church warden, Ralph Benton, reported, "Satan worshipping has gone on. They come from Grimsby in the evenings, light fires, and write symbols on the walls." Occultists have daubed pillars in the church with Satanic graffiti, and evidence suggests that sheep and poultry have been sacrificed. The demonic presence within the church manifests as a dark shadow moving with unnatural speed, accompanied by disembodied footsteps and an unearthly growl. The oppressive atmosphere within St. Botolph's shifts from serene to sinister, leaving visitors with an overwhelming sense of dread.

Clapham Woods, West Sussex

Clapham Woods in West Sussex has long been associated with dark and sinister activities. The woods were famously used as a site of occult rituals by a satanic cult known as the "Friends of Hecate." Detailed in the 1987 book 'The Demonic Connection' by Toyne Newton, Charles Walker, and Alan Brown, this group of Devil worshippers performed animal sacrifices in the woods. Perhaps the most chilling aspect of Clapham Woods is the number of dead bodies that have been found there in recent years. In 1972, a police constable went missing, and his body was later discovered in a patch of brambles. A missing pensioner was found dead in the forest in 1975, the body of a missing reverend was discovered in 1978, and a homeless man was found dead in 1981. The combination of occult activity and unexplained deaths has cemented Clapham Woods' reputation as a site of demonic presence.

Racton Monument, West Sussex

Constructed between 1766 and 1775, the Racton Monument was originally a summerhouse for the 2nd Earl of Halifax, though some believe its true purpose was to watch merchant ships dock at the nearby port village of Emsworth. Abandoned for over a century, the monument fell into disrepair and became a site for multiple suicides and occult rituals. Paranormal investigators frequent the monument, drawn by reports of hauntings and demonic activity. Visitors have claimed to see bricks thrown from above, hear disembodied shouts, and experience an oppressive atmosphere, making Racton Monument a place of both historical interest and dark intrigue.

I invoke thee, Lucifer, from the East, bringer of light and knowledge. Illuminate my path with your wisdom and grant me insight beyond mortal comprehension.

Dark Hexes and Harm

Ritualistic curses—those dark incantations whispered through the veil of shadows—have been woven into the fabric of human fear and fascination for countless ages. As a devoted demonologist, I have seen the aftermath of such curses, their handiwork etched into the lives of those unfortunate enough to be their target.

Victims often report a sense of being watched, a shadowy presence that lurks just beyond the edge of perception. They suffer from inexplicable maladies, a relentless string of bad luck, and a pervasive sense of dread that seeps into every corner of their existence.

But what drives someone to cast such a curse? The reasons are as varied as the curses themselves: revenge, jealousy, the desire for power, or even a misguided attempt to protect. The common thread is a willingness to consort with dark forces, to offer up a piece of one's soul in exchange for the promise of retribution.

Ritualistic curses are born from ancient traditions, often cloaked in secrecy and performed with a chilling precision that underscores their lethal potential. Each word is a key, unlocking gateways to realms unseen and summoning forth entities that hunger for the pain and suffering of the living. The curse, once spoken, latches onto its victim with a tenacity that defies understanding, weaving a web of misfortune, illness, and despair.

As a demonologist, I must stress that cursing someone is not a task to be undertaken lightly, for it involves invoking forces that thrive on chaos and despair. However, in the spirit of illuminating the darkness that shrouds this practice, I shall provide a glimpse into the malevolent art of casting a curse. Beware, for the path you tread may lead to your own undoing.

The Lemon Curse

This ancient and malevolent ritual is not for the faint-hearted. Its potency is legendary, and its results are often chilling. Prepare yourself, for we are about to embark on a journey into the heart of darkness, where curses take shape and demonic forces stir.

First, we must create a cursing oil, a crucial element in our ritual. Begin by selecting your base oil—vegetable, olive, or any similar kind will suffice. Pour a cupful into a pan, the cauldron of our malevolent brew. To this, add a single petal of a black flower, such as a dried black mallow flower, symbolising the dark intent of our spell. For an added touch of lethal potency, sprinkle in a pinch of dried deadly nightshade, but handle with care, for this herb carries the essence of death.

Next, gather a fistful of thorns—five at the very least. These sharp instruments of pain must be added with caution. Add to this concoction a dozen grinds of freshly milled black peppercorns to intensify the heat of your curse. Then, include a generous pinch of ground ginger, or finely chopped fresh ginger if you prefer, to stoke the fires of your dark intentions. Stir this mixture gently, allowing it to meld over a gentle heat for ten minutes. Once brewed, bottle the oil and let it cool. This infernal elixir will be essential in the forthcoming ritual.

Now, prepare yourself for the ritual proper. Ensure your mind is focused and your spirit unwavering. Gather a black candle, a fresh lemon, a bowl, and a photograph of the unfortunate soul you wish to curse.

Begin by lighting the black candle, its flickering flame a beacon in the abyss, focusing your thoughts entirely on your target. With a sharp knife, carve a deep slit into the lemon, creating a vessel for your dark magic. Take the photograph of your intended victim, fold it meticulously while concentrating on your malicious intent, and stuff it deep into the lemon's flesh.

As you do this, speak your intentions aloud, sealing them within the citrus vessel. Each word you utter should resonate with your desire for retribution or malice. Now, take as many rusty nails as you can find, and with each one, stab into the lemon's skin. With every piercing thrust, visualise your target's suffering, feel the curse taking hold, wrapping around them, inescapable and suffocating.

Once the lemon is thoroughly pierced and bristling with rusty nails, place it in a black bowl. Pour your cursing oil over the lemon until it is half-submerged, the oil seeping into the fruit, carrying your curse deep within. Each day, return to the lemon and "feed" it with a drizzle of your cursing oil. This must be done with deliberate intent and unwavering focus. As the lemon rots, decaying into a vile, putrid state, so too will the curse grow in strength and ferocity.

When you sense that the curse has reached its zenith and your vengeance is complete, take the decayed remains of the lemon far from your home and bury it deep in the earth. Let the ground consume what is left, and with it, the remnants of your dark magic.

Thus, the Lemon Curse is fulfilled, its malevolent power unleashed upon the world. Proceed with caution, for the forces you invoke are not to be taken lightly, and the consequences, both seen and unseen, can be dire.

Curse of Eternal Torment

The Curse of Eternal Torment is a powerful and sinister ritual designed to inflict unending suffering upon its target, binding their fate to the darkest forces and ensuring they are plagued by relentless misfortune and despair. The Curse of Eternal Torment draws upon the most malevolent energies, invoking the spirits of the dead and the shadows of the night to achieve its dreadful aim. Proceed with caution, for this curse is not to be taken lightly, and the darkness it calls forth can be unpredictable and perilous.

Begin in a place where shadows cling and light is but a distant memory—a secluded room, preferably underground, where the walls echo with the whispers of forgotten souls. The atmosphere must be thick with the scent of decay, a palpable reminder of the inevitable end that awaits all beings. This is where the malevolent forces you seek to summon will feel at home.

Gather the tools of your dark craft, the instruments of your curse. You will need a black candle, representing the void and the sinister powers you wish to invoke. A piece of parchment will serve as the canvas for your curse, written in your own hand with a quill plucked from a raven and dipped in ink mixed with your own blood, binding the curse to your very essence. An object belonging to your intended victim, something intimate and personal, will act as the anchor for your dark intent. A vial of graveyard dirt is essential, symbolising the connection to the realm of the dead. Finally, you need a dagger, consecrated in a dark ritual, its blade sharp enough to draw blood and sever the ties that bind.

As the midnight hour approaches, when the veil between worlds is at its thinnest, prepare to begin your ritual. Light the black candle, allowing its flickering flame to cast eerie shadows upon the walls. Place the parchment before you and, with the quill, write the name of your target in deliberate, flowing strokes. As you do so, envision their face contorted in fear, their life unravelling in a spiral of torment.

Take the personal item of your victim and wrap it in the parchment, binding it tightly with a piece of black thread. Each knot you tie should be accompanied by a whispered incantation, a dark promise of the suffering you wish to inflict. Let your words be filled with malice, for they will be the vessels of your curse.

Hold the bundle over the flame of the black candle, allowing it to catch fire. As it burns, chant the following invocation:

"By the shadows that dwell in the depths of night,

By the spirits that crave eternal blight,
I call upon the forces dark and deep,
To awaken from their deathless sleep.

(Name), I bind you with this curse I weave,
May your heart be heavy and your soul bereave.
From this day forth, may you know no peace,
Until the day your wretched life does cease."

Scatter the ashes of the burned bundle into the vial of graveyard dirt, sealing it with a drop of your blood. This vial now holds the essence of your curse, a potent vessel of malevolence. Bury it in a place where darkness reigns—beneath a twisted tree, within the confines of a forgotten cemetery, or in the shadow of a desolate ruin.

The curse is now set, a malevolent force that will seep into the life of your target, bringing with it a tide of misfortune and despair. But heed this warning: the forces you have unleashed are capricious and vengeful. They may turn on you if you show the slightest sign of weakness or regret. The path of the curser is fraught with peril, and those who walk it often find themselves ensnared in their own web of darkness.

In the end, to curse another is to dance with demons, to court the abyss that lies beyond the fragile veil of our reality. It is a testament to the darkest aspects of the human soul, a reminder that the shadows we invoke can consume us if we are not careful. Proceed with caution, and always remember that the darkness does not easily forget those who dare to wield its power.

Protection Against Curses

Protection against curses is a delicate and crucial endeavour, for those who find themselves ensnared by dark intentions must take meticulous care to shield their essence from the malevolent forces at play.

The first line of defence against curses is the ritual of purification. These rites serve to cleanse the individual and their surroundings of negative energies, creating a barrier that malevolent forces cannot easily penetrate. Purification rituals often involve the use of sacred herbs such as sage, rosemary, or frankincense, burned to release their purifying smoke. The smoke should be wafted around the person or space, accompanied by a chant or prayer invoking divine protection and cleansing.

Equally vital are protective amulets and talismans, potent tools of protection throughout history. These objects, inscribed with symbols of power and protection like the pentagram, the eye of Horus, or the hamsa hand, serve as physical shields against malevolent forces. One might also carry a piece of black tourmaline or obsidian, stones reputed to absorb and deflect negative energies. These items should be consecrated through a ritual, imbuing them with the intent to shield the bearer from harm. Through these practices, one can erect formidable defences against the malevolent forces that seek to harm, fortified by unwavering belief in their power.

Come forward, forces of darkness, and greet me. Embrace me as your servant and ally in the eternal quest for truth and power. Let your presence be known and felt within this sacred space.

Puppets of Power

"Voodoo dolls," often misunderstood and maligned by the uninformed and media alike, possess a depth and complexity that defy their sinister reputation. These dolls, rooted in diverse cultures and belief systems, serve not merely as instruments of malevolence but as potent tools for healing, protection, and prosperity. The intent behind their use, whether for oneself or another, shapes their purpose.

In the mysterious realm of poppet magic, creating a figure to mirror the recipient of the spell is an art devoid of rigid rules, driven by the practitioner's intention. Inserting pins into these dolls does not necessarily signify pain but may denote the areas where magic is directed. This form of sympathetic magic, the concept that actions upon an effigy can influence the person or object it symbolises, embodies the essence of poppet work.

Poppets, or voodoo dolls, trace their origins to the ancient worlds of Egypt and Greece, but their present image is a tapestry woven from centuries of cultural beliefs. The West African Vodun religion brought forth bocio dolls, wooden figures crafted to attract and contain negative entities for personal gain. In the crucible of slavery, the Hoodoo tradition emerged in the

United States, where gris-gris dolls, employed not for harm but to bestow blessings and fortune, gained prominence. Pins inserted into these dolls served to link them to a person rather than to inflict injury.

Our modern notion of voodoo dolls, influenced by the intersection of Vodun bocio and Hoodoo gris-gris, owes much to European folk magic. The term "poppet," of Old English origin, once denoted a small child or doll and sometimes served as a term of endearment. English tradition wove pins into the fabric of poppet magic, with actions upon the doll believed to affect the person it represented.

The mystique of modern voodoo dolls is steeped in the culture of New Orleans, with the 1932 film 'White Zombie' fusing the dolls with the city's Voodoo culture. Tourism capitalised on this portrayal, birthing a voodoo museum and transforming these dolls into emblems of local mysticism.

Poppet magic transcends the narrow view of harm, finding a place in many witchcraft traditions. These dolls, representing oneself, a friend, a pet, or even an adversary, are conduits for luck, wealth, success, or behavioural influence. The Greeks, for instance, used Kolossoi poppets to restrain malevolent deities or bind lovers. Such traditions touched royalty, with Caroline of Brunswick famously using a poppet against King George IV. West African slaves brought fetish dolls to the

American colonies, where they served as talismans, not as representations of individuals. Post-Civil War, poppets gained a foothold in American Hoodoo and folk magic.

The applications of poppet magic are as varied as human desire—securing a job, ensuring family safety, facilitating healing, attracting love, silencing gossip, or invoking emergency magic. Crafting these poppets involves choosing materials aligned with the desired outcome, imbuing them with herbs and gemstones, and directing energy to the intended goal. The power of poppet magic lies in the intent and focus behind its creation.

Setting clear intentions is paramount in spellwork. These intentions guide the energy channelled into the ritual, harmonising the spell's components. Poppet crafting can range from simple to elaborate, yet sincerity and focus often outweigh complexity. Every element, from materials to symbols, must align with the spell's intent. For instance, a poppet for job security might be fashioned from green fabric, stuffed with clover and chamomile, and adorned with obsidian.

Poppets can serve benevolent purposes like healing or more coercive aims like silencing gossip. Whether created during the ritual or prepared in advance, astrological influences and significant dates can add potency. Visualisation during creation infuses the poppet with intent, the true source of its magic.

The magic of poppets does not reside in their physical form but in the energy, focus, and intent behind their creation. Your belief and intention breathe life into these humble figures, transforming them into potent tools of magic.

Crafting a poppet is an exercise in focus and intent. Choose materials that resonate with your goal—cloth, paper, clay, or wood—manipulated with ease and purpose. If the poppet is to be destroyed after use, select materials that disintegrate naturally. Fabric, often favoured for its versatility, should align in colour with your intention: green or gold for money, black for banishing, white for purity, or red for love.

The poppet's design should bear a resemblance to the person it represents, with basic features like a head, torso, arms, and legs. The creation process may be simple or complex, but hand-sewing over machine sewing infuses the poppet with more intentionality. For a wax poppet, melt candles, let them cool, then shape them. Cloth poppets involve cutting two identical shapes, sewing them together, and stuffing them with appropriate materials—cotton wool, rice, beans, plus symbolic herbs or stones.

Including personal items like hair or nails strengthens the connection, known as taglocks. Symbols that align with your intention, such as astrological signs or numbers, may be inscribed upon the poppet. Consecrate the poppet through prayer or anointment with oil, ensuring that every step is imbued with focus and intention.

To personalise your voodoo doll, decide the influence you wish to exert—thoughts, feelings, or actions. Create a magical link using personal items or symbolic gestures, strengthening the connection. Mimic human features and incorporate magical or astrological symbols to augment the spell's power. Traditional ornaments, crystals, and herbs further enhance the doll's potency, while a written incantation placed inside serves as a constant reminder of the spell's purpose.

A naming ceremony, pinning a photo or writing a name on paper and attaching it to the doll, finalises the bond, readying the doll for spellwork. Personalisation is key to empowering the doll, each step taken with thoughtful intention.

Creating the magical link, or taglock, is crucial. This connection, be it hair, nail clippings, a business card, or a photograph, ties the doll to the individual it represents. Activate the doll by declaring its identity and performing a baptism or naming ceremony if necessary. Purify the doll before activation, using sea salt, incense, or earth energy. Strong, firm words of power bring the doll to life, with anointing oils or waters strengthening the connection.

Perform a binding spell to solidify the bond and recite a protective incantation to empower the doll:

"Majick doll, my little friend.

Away from me all harm you send.

Protect me now through day and night,

as I bless you with this rite.

Blessed by the powers of three.

As I will, So Mote it Be!"

This process transforms your voodoo doll into a potent tool of magic, its power rooted in your intent and the strength of the magical link.

The ritual of creating a voodoo doll demands intention, respect, and focus, ideally conducted under the full moon's watchful gaze. Begin by casting a protective circle, invoking elemental or deity powers. Visualise the desired outcome, guarding the ritual's privacy against negative influences. Magic exacts a price, so be prepared to offer something in return for your desires. Seal the bond with an incantation:

"To the spirit who haunts me,
I cast you into this poppet, no more are you free to roam.
Into the poppet you go, and I control you from now on."

Manipulate the doll to achieve your goals, whether rubbing its eyes for clarity, anointing the crown for wisdom, or piercing the heart to inflict pain. Destroying or locking the doll away can sever the connection or restrain the represented person. After the ritual, wrap the doll in a white cloth and store it safely until the magic manifests, placing it under your pillow for healing or charging it in moonlight. Pins or thorns may be stuck into the doll for specific spell intentions.

The final act in the voodoo doll's journey is its respectful disposal once its purpose is fulfilled. Dismantle the poppet, undoing bindings and removing items to symbolise the release of its connection. Bury the remains to return them to the earth, ensuring complete neutralisation of the contained energies. Sever the magical link with a verbal affirmation:

"Underneath the gaze of the Moon and the Stars,
and by the grace of the Goddess above,
I hereby release this bond,
with heartfelt gratitude and love."

This chant severs the connection, releasing the poppet's energy and intentions, marking the end of its magical purpose.

I invoke thee, Beelzebub, from the North, mighty prince of the infernal empire. Grant me strength and power to overcome all obstacles and adversaries that stand in my way.

Unholy Ceremonies

The Black Mass is a dark and sinister ceremony, shrouded in myth and fear. As a demonologist, I have delved deeply into its origins and practices. This ritual is a twisted parody of the Catholic Mass, intended to mock God and worship the Devil. It is said to involve human sacrifice, obscenity, and blasphemy of the highest order.

The roots of the Black Mass trace back to medieval times, emerging from the fears of witchcraft and demonic pacts. Accounts vary, with some describing elaborate and terrifying rituals, while others dismiss them as mere fabrications. One of the earliest accounts comes from a witch who claimed to have witnessed a Black Mass in France in 1594, involving sixty participants and a blasphemous ceremony performed by a cloaked celebrant.

Central to the Black Mass are sacrilegious elements: wafers made with menstrual blood and semen, wine poured contemptuously on the floor, and missals bound in human skin. The ceremony often features sexual orgies, sacrifices of newborns, and the use of naked bodies as altars. Christian prayers are recited backwards, and candles are made from human fat.

Despite debates and controversies, with some experts claiming the Black Mass to be an illusion, historical figures like the defrocked priest Abbe Boullan are said to have performed these dark rites. Modern interpretations by figures like Aleister Crowley and the Church of Satan use the Black Mass symbolically to reject Christian values rather than to conduct actual rituals.

The Black Mass remains a powerful symbol of defiance against the sacred. Its true nature is obscured by centuries of myth and sensationalism. Yet, as a demonologist, I understand its dark allure and the complex interplay of history, belief, and ritual that surround it. The Black Mass captivates and terrifies, embodying the ultimate rebellion against the divine.

Preparing for a Black Mass is an act drenched in blasphemy and peril, demanding meticulous ritual and a deep understanding of the dark forces at play. As a demonologist, I must emphasise the profound dangers involved. This guidance is shared with utmost caution, and it is vital to be fully aware of the consequences.

Choose your site with care, away from prying eyes and sanctified ground—a decaying church, a hidden cave, or a remote forest glade. The place should exude an aura of decay and desolation to amplify the ritual's potency. Midnight, the witching hour, is the ideal time when the veil between worlds is thinnest.

Transform the ritual space into a setting worthy of dark rites. Drape the altar in black and adorn it with symbols of blasphemy and sacrilege. Surround it with black and red candles, letting their flickering flames cast eerie shadows. The air should be thick with the scent of myrrh, sulphur, and nightshade, creating an oppressive atmosphere.

You will need a chalice, traditionally filled with blood but often substituted with wine or another fitting liquid. A ritual dagger is essential for drawing symbols and making sacrifices. Burn incense and herbs to create an atmosphere thick with the scent of the infernal. Use a piece of bread or a wafer that has been defiled in some manner to mock the sacred Eucharist. Lastly, have a personal journal of dark invocations or individual scripts, containing the precise chants and prayers to be recited.

Select participants with care, ensuring each person is committed to the ritual's purpose and aware of its gravity. Everyone involved should be prepared to partake in every aspect of the ritual, including acts of debasement and sacrifice.

As midnight approaches, gather around the altar and begin the invocation. You may need to attempt Latin or an ancient tongue, as these languages are often used in dark rituals. Raise the chalice, draw symbols with the sacrificial blade, and desecrate the bread or wafer with unerring precision.

Prepare mentally and spiritually, embracing the darkness within and purging yourselves of doubt and fear. Meditate on your intentions and the dark powers you seek to invoke. Engage in preparatory rites such as fasting or abstaining from certain pleasures to heighten your connection to the infernal.

In the most extreme versions, sacrifices may be required to appease the dark forces. These offerings could range from symbolic gestures, such as the destruction of holy objects, to the use of animal or human sacrifices. Make the sacrifice with clear intent and solemn understanding, as it serves as a bridge between the earthly and infernal realms.

Conclude the Black Mass by sealing the ritual. This often involves the consumption of the unholy sacrament and a final invocation of protection for the participants. Cleanse the ritual space and store the implements carefully to ensure the dark forces summoned do not linger.

In conclusion, preparing for a Black Mass is an exercise in profound darkness, demanding absolute commitment and a willingness to embrace the perilous unknown. Those who undertake such rituals tread a path fraught with danger, their souls at risk of being consumed by the very forces they seek to command. Approach with caution, for the shadows are deep and unforgiving.

After conducting a Black Mass, the aftermath is fraught with spiritual peril, and several critical steps must be taken to ensure protection and containment of the dark energies unleashed. As a demonologist, I stress the utmost importance of these measures to prevent malevolent forces from wreaking havoc on your life.

The ritual space must be cleansed immediately. Burn purifying herbs like sage, rosemary, or frankincense, allowing the smoke to permeate every corner. Recite prayers or incantations of purification and protection, invoking benevolent spirits to cleanse and sanctify the area.

Ritual implements must be handled with care. Cleanse the chalice and other tools with salt water or holy water to neutralise any residual negative energies. Ideally, these items should be buried far from your home or ritual space. If burial is not feasible, immerse them in a body of running water to wash away their malevolent associations.

Reflect on the experience and the intentions behind the ritual. Consider the potential consequences of your actions and the impact on your life and others. Use this reflection for growth and understanding, recognising the power and responsibility that come with invoking dark forces.

Remain vigilant for signs of lingering negative influence. Unexplained illnesses, accidents, or feelings of dread may indicate residual energies. If such signs occur, repeat cleansing and protective rituals and seek further spiritual guidance.

Approach the practice of dark rituals with respect and responsibility. The forces you invoke are not to be trifled with, and the consequences can be severe. Treat the spiritual realm with reverence and caution, acknowledging the profound impact of your actions.

By the strength of my spirit and the purity of my will, I draw you out, demon. You are not welcome here. Begone and trouble this soul no more.

Glossary of Terms

Abyss
The bottomless pit often referenced in demonology as the dwelling place of demonic entities, a realm of chaos and darkness.

Altar
A sacred space used in black magic rituals, often adorned with candles, symbols, and offerings to invoke dark forces.

Archdemon
A high-ranking demon, often commanding legions of lesser demons. Known for immense power and influence within the demonic hierarchy.

Attachment
A state where a demon latches onto a person, causing negative influences and gradual possession without full control.

Banishment
A ritualistic expulsion of a demon from a person or location, intended to send the entity back to its realm.

Binding
A powerful incantation or ritual designed to restrict a demon's movements or activities, rendering it powerless.

Black Mass
A sacrilegious ceremony that mocks Christian rituals, often involving the invocation of demons and the desecration of holy symbols.

Blood Magic
A powerful and dangerous form of magic that uses blood, often from a living being, to amplify the potency of spells and rituals.

Candle Magic
A form of ritualistic magic using candles, where different colours represent various intentions and powers, often used in hexes and curses.

Conjuring
The act of summoning a demon through rituals, spells, or invocations.

Covenant
An agreement or pact made between a human and a demon, often involving the exchange of souls or services for power or knowledge.

Curse
A malevolent spell cast to bring harm, misfortune, or death to the target, typically involving ritualistic incantations and symbolic items.

Demon
A malevolent supernatural being associated with evil and hell, frequently involved in possession and destructive rituals in demonology.

Demonic Possession
The phenomenon where a demon inhabits and controls a human body, leading to dramatic changes in behaviour and physical condition.

Demonolatry
The worship and veneration of demons as deities, often involving rituals, sacrifices, and the invocation of their names.

Divination
The practice of seeking knowledge of the future or the unknown through supernatural means, often involving tarot cards, scrying, or runes.

Dybbuks
Malevolent spirits from Jewish folklore that possess living beings, causing harm and distress until exorcised.

Exorcism
The sacred ritual performed to expel a demon from a possessed individual, involving prayers, holy relics, and powerful incantations.

Familiars
Supernatural entities that assist witches and warlocks, often in the form of animals, but in demonology, they are minor demons serving higher-ranked entities.

Gnomes
Earth elementals or nature spirits, traditionally benign but can be invoked in black magic to perform specific tasks or cause harm.

Goetia
A practice within demonology involving the invocation and command of demons, often through the use of specific seals and rituals.

Grimoire
A book of magic spells, rituals, and instructions for invoking and controlling supernatural forces, often passed down through generations.

Hex
A spell cast with the intent to bring bad luck or harm to the target, usually involving symbolic actions and spoken words.

Imps
Small, mischievous demons known for causing minor trouble and pranks, often summoned to do a demon's bidding.

Incantation
A series of words chanted or spoken as a spell or charm to invoke or banish demons.

Infernal Hierarchy
The structured ranking system of demons, from lesser imps to powerful archdemons, each with distinct roles and territories.

Infernal Realm
The domain of demons, often referred to as hell, where evil spirits dwell and originate.

Infestation
The initial phase of a demonic presence in a location, characterised by disturbances and paranormal activity leading up to possession.

Invocation
The act of summoning a demon or demonic force through rituals, chants, and the use of specific symbols or items.

Legion
A group or army of demons, often led by a powerful archdemon, capable of causing widespread chaos and destruction.

Lesser Demons
Minor demonic entities with limited power, often serving more powerful demons or performing specific tasks.

Maleficium
Harmful magic or sorcery, typically involving the summoning of demons to bring about curses, illness, or misfortune.

Manifestation
The physical appearance or presence of a demon in the material world.

Occult
The study of hidden or supernatural forces and beings, often involving rituals, spells, and secret knowledge.

Pact
A formal agreement made with a demon, usually involving the exchange of one's soul or services for demonic power or knowledge.

Pentacle
A protective symbol often used in rituals to summon or repel demons, typically a five-pointed star within a circle.

Poppet
A doll used in sympathetic magic, representing a person to whom the caster wishes to direct their spells, either for harm or healing.

Ritual
A series of actions or words performed in a set sequence, often for religious or magical purposes.

Runes
Ancient symbols used in divination and magic, each rune holding specific meanings and powers, often carved into objects or drawn on surfaces.

Sex Magic
A form of magical practice that uses sexual energy and acts to empower rituals and spells, often involving the invocation of spirits or demons.

Scrying
A method of divination involving gazing into a reflective surface, such as a mirror, crystal ball, or water, to receive visions or messages.

Sigil
A symbol believed to have magical power, often used in rituals to summon or control demons.

Spell
A ritualistic set of actions, words, and symbols designed to produce a magical effect, ranging from love spells to curses.

Succubus/Incubus
Demons that seduce humans in their dreams, feeding off their life force. A succubus is female, and an incubus is male.

Summoning
The act of calling forth a demon through specific rituals or incantations.

Talisman
An object believed to contain magical properties that bring good luck or protection to the bearer, often created and charged through rituals.

Theurgy
The practice of invoking demons or supernatural beings to achieve spiritual enlightenment or material gain, often involving complex rituals.

Warding
The act of creating protective barriers, often through the use of symbols, charms, or incantations, to repel demonic entities.

Witch Bottle
A protective charm filled with various items, such as herbs, nails, and bodily fluids, intended to ward off evil spirits and curses.

Witchcraft
The practice of magical arts involving spells, rituals, and the invocation of supernatural powers, often associated with both benevolent and malevolent intentions.

Witching Hour
The time of night, typically around midnight, when supernatural activity is believed to be at its peak.

Printed in Great Britain
by Amazon

79a752c3-15e6-49f3-8a64-cd1b82cda7b7R01